HOME OFFICE RESEARCH STUDY NO. 83

Parental Supervision and Juvenile Delinquency

by David Riley and Margaret Shaw

A HOME OFFICE
RESEARCH AND PLANNING UNIT
REPORT

LONDON: HER MAJESTY'S STATIONERY OFFICE

HOME OFFICE RESEARCH STUDIES

'Home Office Research Studies' comprise reports on research undertaken in the Home Office to assist in the exercise of its administrative functions, and for the information of the judicature, the services for which the Home Secretary has responsibility (direct or indirect) and the general public.

On the last pages of this report are listed titles already published in this series, in the preceding series of *Studies in the Causes of Delinquency and the Treatment of Offenders,* and in the series of *Research and Planning Unit Papers.*

Her Majesty's Stationery Office

Standing order service

Placing a standing order with HMSO BOOKS enables a customer to receive other titles in this series automatically as published.

This saves the time, trouble and expense of placing individual orders and avoids the problem of knowing when to do so.

For details please write to HMSO BOOKS (PC 13A/1), Publication Centre, PO Box 276, London SW8 5DT and quoting reference X25.08.07.

The standing order service also enables customers to receive automatically as published all material of their choice which additionally saves extensive catalogue research. The scope and selectivity of the service has been extended by new techniques, and there are more than 3,500 classifications to choose from. A special leaflet describing the service in detail may be obtained on request.

Foreword

Earlier studies in the present series by Martin Davies (No.2) and by Ian Sinclair (No.6) stressed the role of family relationships and, in particular, firm but kindly discipline in predicting the success of teenagers on probation. More generally, it has been found in a wide variety of research that the nature of the supervision exercised by parents is an important factor in delinquency. This may have preventive implications in that if the ingredients of successful supervison could be identified they might be communicated in the form of advice to parents.

The present study provides an up-to-date account of the association between parental control and juvenile offending, in the context of a nationally-representative survey based on interviews with both teenagers and their parents. The effects of supervision are considered in the framework of competing influences on delinquency and it is concluded that parents are still able to make an effective contribution to their children's conduct outside the home. The final chapter contains a number of suggestions which some parents might find helpful.

MARY TUCK
Deputy Head of the Research and Planning Unit

Acknowledgements

We would like to thank all the parents and teenagers who took part in the survey — it was their interest and willingness to discuss their experiences which gave life to the study. We hope they will find it to have been worthwhile. Our thanks for their very crucial role in helping to shape the project go to Douglas Wood and his staff at Social and Community Planning Research, and to David Farrington who acted as a consultant and Clive Payne who gave us useful help with the analyses. Any defects in the report remain, of course, the responsibility of the authors. We also wish to thank Ron Clarke for the inspiration and the opportunity to embark on the study, Nicholas Dorn for advice on alcohol and drugs and Michael Gottfredson for his valuable comments on the preparation of this report.

DAVID RILEY

MARGARET SHAW

Contents

Diff between boys & Girls

PEERS ALSO

1 Introduction

Family life and the lives of young teenagers are thought to have changed a great deal over past years. But it is not always clear whether the changes are as great as is sometimes made out. There is often a tendency for people to look back to their own childhood or to an earlier era as a golden age (Pearson, 1983). Nevertheless, young people nowadays would appear to have more money and material possessions and more autonomy than their predecessors. There also seem to be more opportunities for them to get into difficulties and perhaps more pressures on them to do so. Increases in football hooliganism, vandalism and shoplifting, and more recently in drug taking and drinking among teenagers have been well publicised. In such circumstances parents and teenagers themselves may find it difficult to know how to deal with situations which are new to both of them. Many parents may be unsure about how far they should intervene or let their children make their own decisions. Yet there is often little doubt in the minds of the public that it is parents who are to blame when things go wrong.

When asked what are the main causes of juvenile crime most people will mention lack of discipline by parents. Some 70–90% of respondents have done so in surveys in this country over the past 20 years or more, and in a number of cases it has been seen as the main cause (Banks *et al.*, 1975; Research Bureau Limited, 1979). Most people's notion of parental discipline involves some element of supervision. Some parents may be seen as too easy-going or permissive, or as indifferent to their children's activities. Others may be seen as too restrictive or erratic in the extent to which they try to govern the behaviour of their children. Yet how far is it possible to lay down generally acceptable guidelines about how parents should supervise their children? Such supervision must in a sense be a matter of personal choice. It must also be influenced by other factors in the life of the family such as how much time parents have to spend with their children, and the circumstances of their daily lives.

It may be that our present day society must accept that a certain amount of delinquency will occur, however much effort we put into identifying potential delinquents or changing the kind of circumstances which are associated with delinquency. Delinquency occurs in almost all societies and in conditions of prosperity as well as decline. Similarly, no one intervention is likely to reduce delinquency overnight and finding the resources to provide aid on all fronts never seems feasible. But we may in a small way be able to reduce the chances of it occurring by paying more attention to what goes on at the family level

INTRO

1

before or at least during the period when delinquent behaviour is most prevalent. The importance of the school, the influence of other teenagers, or of poor social and economic conditions cannot be overlooked, but there are a number of reasons why it may also be worth looking again at the part which families can play as their children reach their early teens.

This report is based on a national survey of young teenagers of 14 and 15 and their parents. It was designed to explore the extent to which supervision is exercised by parents, and the part it plays in preventing delinquency. It offers some insight into the relationships which exist between parents and their children in their early teens. And it raises issues about the responsibilities of both sides in relation to delinquency.

The family and delinquency

Children at 14 or 15 do not officially have a great deal of autonomy, being legally still subject to parental and educational authority, yet they form the peak ages for officially recorded offending.

Both official data on convictions and cautions and self-report studies based on admissions of delinquent behaviour have shown that delinquent activity tends to increase from about the age of 12 reaching a peak at 14 or 15 (Figure 1) and thereafter declines (see, for example, Rutter and Giller, 1983).

Self-report studies have also helped to demonstrate that delinquent behaviour, much of which is relatively trivial, is very common among children. Such studies have also shown that some delinquent behaviour is to be found among children from all kinds of backgrounds, but that only a very small minority are ever caught or prosecuted (Belson, 1975; Shapland, 1978).

Interest in the role of the family in preventing delinquency is not new. Some 50 years of research has established without much doubt that children who begin offending at an early age and who become serious offenders tend to come from large families, to have parents with a criminal record, to have poor or erratic discipline at home, conflict between parents, and poor supervision by their parents (Glueck and Glueck, 1950; West and Farrington, 1973 and 1977; Wadsworth, 1979). But most of this research has based its conclusions on assessments of family circumstances and relationships when the children are young rather than during their early teens (although West and Farrington had family measures at 14–15), and almost all has focused on boys since they are more likely to find themselves before the courts than girls. Yet while there is no doubt a relationship between such family features and serious delinquency, most delinquent behaviour is not of this kind. It can be argued, therefore, that our understanding of delinquency and of the role of parental supervision would be extended by looking at a wider range of families and circumstances than has been the case to date (Rutter and Giller, 1983).

2

Figure 1
Persons found guilty or cautioned in England and Wales for indictable offences:
number *per* 100,000 population in the age group

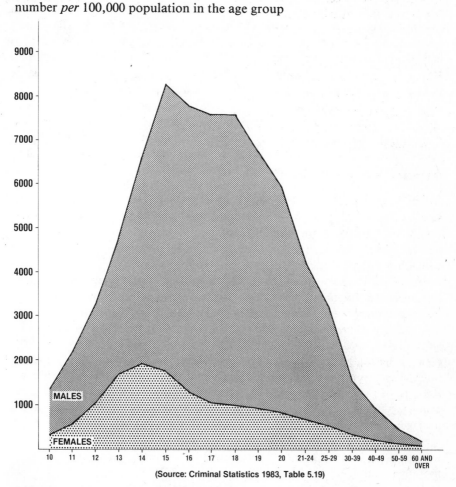

(Source: Criminal Statistics 1983, Table 5.19)

Previous research on parental supervision

Parental supervision is one of the few family factors which has consistently been found to be associated with delinquency. One influential American study published in 1950 included unsuitable supervision by mothers as one of five key factors identifying future delinquents (Glueck and Glueck, 1950). Parental supervision has usually been measured by a combination of factors. These have included such items as how much free time a child spends out of the home, how far parents have rules about what the child is allowed to do or where they can go, or the time they must come home at night. They have often included rules about such things as bed times and doing jobs about the house, and some estimate of the extent to which rules are enforced. The study of boys growing up in inner London (West and Farrington, 1973) included an

3

assessment of parental supervision when they were aged 8 or 9. Parents of many of the delinquents in the study "were less concerned than other parents to watch over or know about their children's doings, whereabouts and companions, and they failed to enforce or to formulate fixed rules about such things as punctuality, manners, bedtime, television viewing or tidying up" (West, 1982). Boys who were poorly supervised at that age were more likely to become delinquent subsequently than those from families where supervision was good. Poor supervision, however, was more common among large families, the poorer families, and those where parents themselves had a criminal history. Such factors may have contributed both to parents' ability to supervise their children and to the chances of them becoming delinquent. The conclusion remains, nevertheless, as one of the authors has put it that: "poor supervision could be one of the most important ways in which parents fail to protect their sons from delinquency" (West, 1982).

A series of studies by Harriett Wilson has looked closely at parental supervision of groups of boys at 3 and 4, at 6 and 7 and at 10 and 11 years. They were all from poor families living in high crime areas in the Midlands. She concluded that even among families with large numbers of children and facing considerable hardship, boys who were poorly supervised were more likely to be delinquent than those well supervised. In her view, nevertheless, the difficulties of coping with the stresses brought about by low income, poor living conditions and large families make it very difficult for parents to exercise good supervision (Wilson and Herbert, 1978; Wilson, 1980 and 1982).

Both of the studies referred to here have concentrated on boys living in poorer inner-city or suburban areas of England and Wales where rates of crime are likely to be high, and upon parents' attempts to supervise them from an early age or up to about 10 or 11 years. But what about supervision among young teenagers, when absence from direct parental supervision is likely to be much greater? Some evidence comes from a study of 11–15 year old boys in Liverpool which found that boys spending long hours on the streets reported more vandalism than others (Gladstone, 1978). An American study of secondary school children between 12 and 17 also using self-report techniques found that boys whose mothers usually knew where they were were less likely to report delinquent behaviour than others. It was also found that delinquency was lower among boys who had close ties with their parents and who were on good terms with their father, and the study suggests that boys' attachment to their families helps to protect them from delinquency. The family bonds act as a form of social control (Hirschi, 1969). Such findings are paralleled by research in this country on the characteristics of probationer's families and probation hostel wardens which seem to predict success (Davies, 1969; Sinclair, 1971). Firm but affectionate or kindly relationships between fathers and sons or between hostel wardens and their residents were found to be the most successful in preventing reconvictions. Similarly, Lewis, Newson and Newson (1982) found that children in their birth cohort who had had good

ROLE OF FATHER

relations with their fathers as they reached adolescence were relatively unlikely to acquire a criminal record.

On the whole, however, not a great deal is known about supervision practices among parents of older children, almost nothing is known about girls (although Campbell, 1981 provides some recent evidence), and most of our information in this country comes from studies of children living in poorer urban areas. Much research into delinquency has tended to stress that it is early life experiences which influence subsequent behaviour, and to assume that it may be too late to alter behaviour by the early teens. More recently it has been argued that there is a need for continued and consistent social learning throughout childhood and early adolescence — and that a happy and secure childhood is not sufficient in itself — to prevent subsequent delinquency (West, 1982). Additionally, there is a large body of evidence which points to the importance of opportunity in the commission of delinquency (Mayhew, Clarke, Sturman and Hough, 1976; Cohen and Felson, 1979). Other evidence points to the lessening of parental contact with teenagers (Felson and Gottfredson, 1984). Young teenagers are presented with far greater opportunities to offend than their younger brothers and sisters, and clearly many take them. If there are also more opportunities to offend than in the past then perhaps parents need to be more aware of this.

Renewed interest in the family

Concern about juvenile offending has been matched in recent years with concern about the changes taking place in family life which some see as evidence that the family is a declining institution. There have been increases in marriage breakdown and divorce, in re-marriage, in the numbers of one-parent families, in the numbers of working mothers (Rimmer, 1981; Study Commission on the Family, 1982; Willmott and Willmott, 1982). Many of these changes have accelerated during the 1970s, following the Divorce Reform Act 1969 (which took effect in 1971), for example, and over the same period there have been substantial increases in the proportion of mothers who work outside the home. Such changes in family composition and function have led to a concern about their effects on delinquency although not for the first time (see Smelser, 1982 and Pearson, 1983 for example). Interest in the family has not, however, been restricted to what may be seen as negative aspects. It has become clear, for example, that the family plays a central role in the educational achievements of children, and that better relationships between parents and school are in the interests of both.

The renewal of interest in the family's role in delinquency prevention is also reflected in the 1982 Criminal Justice Act which incorporates a number of provisions designed to bring home to parents their legal responsibility for their children's behaviour. These include being responsible for paying their fines up to the age of 17, and paying compensation or being bound over to ensure that their children are subject to proper control. The same Act has also provided

5

magistrates with powers to restrict the activities of juveniles between 6pm at night and 6am, when they can be ordered to stay at home. Thus the stress on parental responsibility for their children's actions is also coupled with renewed interest in supervising those activities.

It seems appropriate, in view of these developments, to look at family supervision practices across a wide range of families living in a variety of circumstances, and to look at the period when delinquent activity is at its peak. From the point of view of teenagers and their parents it may be helpful to know what other families do and think. From the point of view of policy-makers it would be helpful to know more about what seems to 'work', since so much information about offending tends to be derived from our knowledge of cases where things appear to have 'gone wrong' in some way.

The present study

Since the study was designed to provide a broad view of supervision among families of young teenagers, it took the form of a national survey based on households in England and Wales. (As with any survey, the fact that not all those contacted agreed to take part must raise questions about the representa-tiveness of the sample finally studied. It is possible that families with children more involved in delinquency were also more likely to refuse to take part and this must be borne in mind.) Successful interviews were completed with 751 families with a teenager of 14 or 15 (a 73% response rate) — 373 of them girls and 378 of them boys. Interviews were conducted by an independent survey organisation, Social & Community Planning Research, and took place between June and August 1983. Details of the method used to select the sample, screening and interviewing techniques are given in Appendix 1.

Interviews were held separately with the mother and the teenager in each family. Where no mother was living in the household, the father was seen. (It had been hoped to interview fathers too to obtain a more balanced picture of parents' views on supervision. Experience during the developmental stage of the project sugggested that this would be both costly and difficult to accomplish satisfactorily: see Appendix 1.) Interviews with the parent lasted about 45 minutes and those with the teenager about 30 minutes.

The survey covered a wide range of questions concerning family life in relation to the teenager. These included aspects of supervision and the extent of family discussion and interaction. The kinds of issues about which parents had arguments with their teenagers or about which they gave advice were explored. The teenagers were asked a similar range of questions about how they spent their time both in the home and outside. They were asked about school and friends, and about how well they got on with their parents. Their attitudes to offending and such things as smoking, drinking and drugs were explored. Finally, they were asked whether they had ever committed a range of minor and more serious acts of behaviour which would be defined as offences if they were caught. This information provided a measure of self-reported offending. It was used to assess the extent to which the supervision which parents exercised seemed to have an effect upon the activities of their teenage children.

Plan of the report

It is always difficult in a large survey to do justice to the complexity of people's lives. What this report attempts to do is to give an overall picture of the lives of the 751 families interviewed in relation to the question of supervision. Chapter 2 deals with the views of the parents and how they see their role in bringing up teenagers. Chapter 3 considers supervision from the point of view of the teenagers themselves. It discusses the way they spend their time and their relationships with their friends and family and attempts to assess the scope for better supervision. Chapter 4 deals with the relationship between delinquency and the supervision exercised by parents. Chapter 5 considers aspects of parental supervision in more detail. Chapter 6 is concerned with the one-parent families in the survey and more generally with the problems of living under conditions of stress. The final chapter attempts to draw together the findings of the study and assesses what more could be done to help both parents and teenagers to reduce the chances of delinquency among this age group.

2 The parents' view

Parents who work?

For some parents coping with adolescent children is often difficult. While facilities such as pre-school play groups or mother and baby clinics provide parents with support in coping with young children, such facilities are less obviously available for the parents of teenagers. They are assumed to have learnt how to deal with their children.

To some extent it can be argued that the need for such support is a relatively new problem. Compulsory schooling and a high school-leaving age have extended the period of dependence on the family (Smelser, 1982). Yet changing working patterns, among other factors, have reduced the amount of time and perhaps energy which parents have to cope with their families (Willmott and Willmott, 1982). Far more mothers now work at least part-time than was the case 30 years ago for example. They comprised 12% of the workforce in 1951, compared with 26% by 1979 (Rimmer and Popay, 1982). And one American writer has suggested that the difficulties which parents often face in dealing with their children are less the result of greater permissiveness than simply of having less time and less contact with their families (Bronfenbrenner, 1971). Indeed there is some American evidence that older teenagers now spend less time in the company of parents or other adults than was the case for previous generations (Felson and Gottfredson, 1984).

This chapter is based upon interviews with the parents of teenagers (733 mothers and 18 fathers). (Where mothers were interviewed care was taken to ask them also about fathers' views on the issues discussed.) It examines parents' capacities to exercise direct supervision in terms of how much time they had to spend with their teenagers and how far they maintained less direct forms of supervision or control. It also describes the kinds of issues over which they had disagreements or gave advice. The majority of the teenagers in the survey were living in two-parent households — only 12% in a single-parent household — and for the most part this section is concerned with the more prevalent situation. (Chapter 6 considers single-parents and their teenagers.)

Working patterns and supervision

How much scope was there for parents to supervise their teenagers' free time directly? As children grow up there is an increasing tendency for mothers to work. For example, the Study Commission on the Family (1982) reported that

8

by the time their youngest child is 10 years of age, some 70% of mothers will be working. Eighty-seven per cent of the fathers in the survey were working at the time of the interview, and as many as two-thirds of the mothers (see Table 1). Of the mothers in the survey who worked, three-quarters did so on a part-time basis.

Table 1
Employment status of respondents and their partners

Employment status	Mothers (N = 729)	Fathers (N = 675)
In full-time work	23%	87%
In part-time work: 10 hours or less per week	33%	< 1%
10 or more hours per week	9%	< 1%
Not in or seeking work	33%	5%
Seeking work	3%	8%

Generally, at least one parent was at home when the teenager left for school, and most (83%) of the teenagers said there was usually an adult at home when they arrived back from school. (However, it is not known how parents coped during school holidays.) In spite of the increases in employment among mothers, therefore, there seemed little evidence from this survey that teenagers were left to themselves before and after school during school terms. Indeed the fact that a mother worked was not found to be related to delinquency (a similiar finding was reported by Gladstone, 1978, while West and Farrington (1973) found less delinquency among boys whose mothers were working).

While parents may have less time for family interaction than previously, two-thirds of the mothers in the survey were, nevertheless, reasonably content with the amount of time which they had available to spend with their child. Fathers were less content — almost half of them would have preferred to spend more time with their son or daughter, and the majority (80%) of these fathers blamed work or the unsocial hours which they had to keep, while about a fifth said their teenager was usually otherwise engaged. Indeed about half (54% of the boys and 44% of the girls) were reported by their parents to go out "a lot" in their free time.

Supervising the teenager

Supervision cannot always take the form of direct contact with parents. They must rely upon other ways of monitoring or attempting to control the activities of their teenagers when away from home. The fact that parents know where their children are has been taken by one researcher to indicate 'virtual' supervision of their activities — the children in a sense 'took their parents with them' when they went out (Hirschi, 1969). Concern about where their teenagers would be and what they would be up to did seem to be central to the families in the present survey (see Table 2). Most parents (79%) "almost always" asked their teenager where they were going when they went out in their spare time, and 76% who with. However, they were less likely to know *what* they would be doing — indeed only half the boys' parents thought they generally knew what they did.

Table 2
Parents' knowledge of teenagers' out of home activities[1]

Proportion of parents who say they "almost always" know...	Boys (N = 378)	Girls (N = 373)
..where they are	76%	83%
..who they are with	72%	82%
..what they are doing	53%	64%

Not surprisingly, there was a considerable divergence of opinion between the parents and the teenagers about how much they knew about their activities. Only 48% of the boys said their parents "almost always" knew where they were, and 31% what they were doing. There was little disagreement about who they were with. Among the girls too there were discrepancies which suggested that parents did not know where they were or what they were doing as often as they assumed.

Yet almost all parents (94%) thought they *should* know what their children were up to when they were out and the overwhelming majority felt strongly about this (see Table 3). There was only a small proportion who felt that this was not necessary because by this age children should be allowed some privacy, or were to be trusted without the need for questions:

She must be allowed some privacy. You can't live their lives for them — you bring them up properly and hope they will have respect for you.

I trust him. You needn't know what he's doing if you trust him.

But such confidence was not universal and 40% of the parents worried about what their teenagers were up to when they were out.

[1]Unless otherwise stated percentages given in subsequent tables are based on the numbers of boys and girls shown in this table.

Table 3
Going out: parents and their teenagers

	Boys	Girls
Parents "almost always" trust teenager to behave when out with friends	78%	85%
Teenager "almost always" willing to give details of spare time activities	67%	76%
Parents feel strongly that they should know about how their teenager spends his/her spare time	84%	86%
Parents worry about what their teenager might get up to	39%	41%

What was evident among many parents, was an underlying worry about what they might be up to, or about the harm they might come to, but coupled with an overall feeling that they should or could trust their son or daughter to behave well when they were out: "I like to know who she is with, where she is going and how she is going to get home — because it isn't safe for young girls to go around on their own in the evenings. I don't necessarily want to know what they are doing because I can trust her to behave herself." There was too a feeling that too many restrictions could have the wrong effect: "...if you tie them down you have problems." 'Supervision' for most of the parents at this age, therefore, was based upon a concept of trust. It was evident, however, that different standards of supervision were being applied to boys and girls. Parents were much stricter about asking girls where they were going, and with whom, than boys. *maybe why more*

One of the most important issues for the parents seemed to centre around times for coming home at night. These varied considerably and probably reflected local conditions (eg transport facilities) as well as parents' views of appropriate hours (see Table 4). *boys are delinquent!*

Most were expected home between 9 and 10pm in the week and rather later at weekends — in half the cases 10pm or later. In the case of girls this was 'almost always' fixed before they went out, but less so for boys. Most parents (90%) felt they could trust their child to come home at a sensible time if arrangements had not been made beforehand.

11

Table 4
Latest time teenagers normally expected home
(a) During the week

	Boys	Girls
Before 9pm	17%	19%
9pm to 9.59pm	48%	47%
10pm to 10.59pm	29%	31%
11pm or later	6%	3%

(b) At the weekend

	Boys	Girls
Before 9pm	11%	12%
9pm to 9.59pm	37%	37%
10pm to 10.59pm	37%	37%
11pm or later	15%	13%

Supervising friends $PEERS$

The friends which teenagers have — as subsequent chapters will discuss — seem to exert a powerful effect upon their behaviour. Many parents will complain that it is friends who get a child into trouble. How far do parents know who their children's friends are, or attempt to influence their choice of friends? About half of the parents thought they knew by name almost all of them, and another third most of them. Yet knowing their names may not be sufficient. The now common pattern of large secondary schools with big catchment areas makes it likely that parents will not actually have met all of the friends: one parent's knowledge was limited to discussions with her child about school friends — she had never actually met any of them. Few parents felt the need to attempt to control choice of friends: two-thirds of them had not found reason to disapprove of *any* of their child's friends over the past three years and only one in eleven (9%)currently did so. In such cases most parents were still prepared to take steps to persuade their child not to spend time with them.

Agreements and disagreements: winning in the short-term?

The survey as a whole did not show adolescence to be an invariable period of "storm and stress" (Murdock, 1979). Many of the parents accepted that they had less direct control over their children's activities than previously. They recognized that their teenagers were at times less communicative than in the past and needed more privacy and independence in order to grow up. Most parents were still exercising a fair degree of authority, however, and this was not strongly disputed by the teenagers. Disagreements were common but not serious, and serious rows rare — only 11% of parents reporting them. About half the parents reported occasional disagreements about general appearance, clothes and hair styles — rather more with boys than with girls and only 15% or so had arguments about pocket money. Fewer than one in four parents mentioned disagreements about where their children were allowed to go, with whom or what they would be doing (Table 5).

Table 5
Parents' account of disagreements with their teenagers

Proportion of parents having disagreements about...	Boys	Girls
where they are	16%	21%
the friends they spend time with	17%	15%
what they get up to with their friends	11%	6%

Table 6
Tellings off and other sanctions
(a) Frequency of tellings off

	Boys	Girls
Never	11%	13%
Once a fortnight or less	31%	38%
Once a week	22%	21%
2–3 times a week	22%	21%
4 or more times a week	14%	7%

(b) Other sanctions (in the last six months)

Keeping in	11%	11%
Setting curfew	1%	2%
Stopping pocket money	4%	3%
Hitting	10%	7%

Over half the teenagers occasionally complained that their friends were allowed greater freedom than themselves. On the whole, parents seemed still to be winning what disputes there were, or rather more often, a compromise was reached. Parental authority was also demonstrated by the imposition of sanctions. Twenty per cent had imposed specific sanctions on their children in the past six months (Table 6). In most cases this involved stopping them from going out, but occasionally hitting them or stopping pocket money. And rather more parents (88%) had to reprimand their child from time to time, often about once or twice a week.

The parents' view of school

Because so much of a child's life evolves around school, it plays a large part in family discussion, and was something about which almost all teenagers sought their parents' advice. Most of the parents seemed content with their teenager's school, and the standards of teaching, but 33% felt that discipline could be stricter. Eighty-five per cent had visited the school at least once within the last year, mainly to discuss their child's progress and a quarter to discuss problems of their child's behaviour (Table 7).

Table 7
Parents' visits to their teenagers' school over the past year to talk to teachers
(a) Number of visits

	Boys	Girls
None	16%	15%
1	36%	35%
2–3	42%	44%
4 or more	6%	6%

(b) Reasons for visits

	Boys	Girls
General progress at school	69%	72%
Behaviour at school	5%	3%
Both progess and behaviour	23%	21%
Other reasons	3%	4%

Homework appeared to be a common source of friction for parents: almost half of the boys needed to be pushed to do it, compared with a quarter of the girls, and to do it more carefully. Truanting and behavioural problems at school were not — in the parents' view — common among the sample: 11% of the parents reported their children had played truant. However, almost twice as many of the teenagers said they had stayed away from school when they should have been there.

Disagreements between parents

Much delinquency research has stressed the importance of consistency between

14

parents in bringing up children, as well as the damaging effects of serious marital discord (for a review see Rutter and Giller, 1983). The present study had to rely upon mothers, as the primary parental respondent, to report the views of their spouses. While the survey did not specifically attempt to assess the amount of serious discord between parents, over half the parents reported occasional disagreements between themselves about what the teenager should be allowed to do. Mothers on the whole were thought by their children to be less restrictive than fathers, and about two-fifths of the teenagers were inclined to play one parent off against the other.

Smoking, drinking and drugs

A number of studies in recent years have been concerned with increases in smoking and drinking among young people (Bynner, 1969; OPCS, 1983; Fogelman, 1978). There is also some evidence and widespread concern about increases in drug use and glue sniffing among children of this age (eg. Dorn and Thompson, 1975; Black, 1982). How far are parents of 14 and 15 year-olds concerned to control or influence their children's behaviour on these issues?

Drinking was clearly acceptable — 84% of the parents had allowed their child to have an alcoholic drink, usually at home or on a special occasion, at some time. About a third of the parents reported that their son or daughter had also drunk alcohol when they were not present, but with their knowledge — a fact supported by almost all the teenagers who claimed that their parents were aware when they had had a drink. Drinking in less controlled situations than family gatherings was less well endorsed by the parents. Three-quarters of them would definitely not allow alcohol at a party for young people of 14 or 15 at home, although half of them would allow their teenager to go to such a party elsewhere. There did not seem too much concern about drinking on the whole. About a quarter reported their son or daughter had been drinking without their consent, and were upset about it. Even so, less than half the parents (45%) had ever specifically discussed drinking with the teenager in question. (See Table 8.)

Smoking was far less acceptable to parents: even though just under two-thirds of the parents smoked themselves. Almost 70% had given their son or daughter advice about it and only 9% reported that their child smoked now, although a third were aware that they had tried a cigarette at some stage. Most parents reported they would be very upset to find them smoking and would take action if they did. Slightly more teenagers (11%) had reported they were current smokers, and their own estimates of the number of cigarettes they smoked — many of them reporting between 20 and 40 a week — were well above their parents' estimates.

15

Table 8
Parental advice about smoking, drinking, drugs and sex

Given advice about	Boys	Girls
Smoking	69%	68%
Drinking	44%	46%
Sex	53%	73%
Drugs	70%	67%

Drugs and glue sniffing were also things about which parents were clearly concerned. Just under 70% had given advice about them or discussed them with their son or daughter (Table 8). Very few of the teenagers, however, admitted having used any, although about 18% of them had been offered glue, cannabis or pills, and 40% knew someone who had taken some of these substances.

Parental concern about sexual relationships was also evident, but again showing a marked distinction between the parents of boys and girls: three-quarters of the girls' parents but only half of the boys' had discussed sex and relations with boy or girl friends with their teenager.

Getting into trouble with the police

Crime was a subject about which most parents had views. In keeping with surveys of the general public discussed in Chapter 1, the most frequent reason given by the parents for young people getting into trouble with the police was lack of parental interest or control. Parents were thought not to discipline their children, to let them stay out long hours, or to do as they liked, or simply to be uninterested in them. The second most common explanation was boredom: such young people had nothing to do and no facilities existed for them. (It was of interest that the teenagers' own explanation of why young people got into trouble stressed the desire for 'kicks' — to make themselves feel big or to show off to peers — rather more than boredom or lack of parental control.)

Fifteen per cent of the parents reported that their child had at some time done something which could have got them in trouble with the police, and in two out of three of these cases the police had been involved. Most of these parents had been extremely upset. Yet parents were perhaps underestimating the extent to which the teenagers might get into trouble with the police. Three-quarters of them thought it very unlikely that this would happen within the next two years, but as the discussion of self-report offending in Chapter 4 will show — just under half of the teenagers reported having recently committed an act which *could* get them into trouble. A corresponding discrepancy was evident from

16

parents' reports of delinquent behaviour on the part of their children's friends. In only 13% of the cases did parents know that friends had committed delinquent acts, whereas more than two-thirds of the teenagers reported they had.

Two sections of the Criminal Justice Act 1982 affect parents in stressing their responsibility for the actions of their children, and parents were asked their views about them. Ninety per cent thought that the imposition of a night restriction order (which enables magistrates to order a juvenile to stay at home at a specified time between 6pm and 6am, and for up to 30 days as part of a Supervision Order) was a good innovation. Only 5% of parents said they would not agree to it, but rather more (14%) thought it would be difficult to enforce:

> I don't think it would help the situation. A lot of offences can be done before 6pm and I think it may even cause harm. It could make them want to disappear altogether. They would still get out through a window... they would then do something worse perhaps.

Parents were less enthusiastic about the court's powers to order them to pay fines (or compensation) if their children were in trouble. One third of the parents did not think this a useful innovation, either because it would fail to teach children a lesson, or because it was seen as unfair on the parents. They could not be wholly responsible for their children's actions. The majority of parents though were positive about the new provisions.

Summary

(handwritten note: link to Parenting order)

This chapter has been concerned with patterns of parental involvement, supervision and control among the families surveyed. These were factors thought to be relevant to the prevention of delinquent behaviour among young teenagers. It would appear that boys are subject to less supervision than girls and to different parental expectations about their behaviour. They are, however, also less likely to keep to parents' expectations and require more chivying. Some parents, particularly fathers, feel they are not able to spend as much time with their teenage children as they would wish. Parents are still using sanctions as a way of keeping behaviour within the limits defined by them, and there is evidence of negotiation between parents and children at this age. But on the whole there are few serious disagreements. Parents clearly worry about the activities of their teenagers, and they are not as well informed about them as they think they are. Few feel the need to control their child's choice of friends. The implications of some of these findings will be considered at the end of the report in Chapter 7.

3 The teenagers' view

At 14 and 15 teenagers are well into the transition phase from childhood and dependence to a more independent and autonomous life-style. For some, the transition takes a long time and often the teenagers in the study had life-styles and habits much more in keeping with younger age groups. Others were more mature than their age might imply. This chapter is concerned with aspects of the lives of the young people in the study including what they do with their time. It thus deals in part with the scope which exists for delinquency prevention. Most delinquent acts will, after all, take place away from home and school and the way in which young teenagers use their spare time may be as important as the amount which they have.

Apart from assessing the opportunities which exist for teenagers to commit offences in the absence of adult oversight, however, it is also important to examine the extent to which they still feel themselves to be part of their families. It has been argued, as the discussion in Chapter 1 indicated, that it is closeness and attachment to the family which helps to guide children's actions when they are away from their parents (Hirschi, 1969). To what extent, therefore, did the teenagers in the survey spend time with their families and feel attached to them, and to what extent did they appear to associate and identify with their peer group?

Three aspects of their lives are considered: their use of free time, including involvement with clubs and organized activities, who they spend their time with and where; secondly their spending habits, sources of money and views on certain aspects of their lives; and thirdly their involvement with their parents, in terms of how close they felt to them and how much time they still spent talking or doing things together. A final section is concerned with their reactions to supervision and the extent to which they felt that their parents' practices were fair.

What teenagers do with their time: organized activities

Most teenagers have a number of options to choose from in their use of free time: to spend it alone, with friends, with their families, or to be involved in organized activities. How they spend it (and indeed the amount which they have) will in part be determined by parental influence. The availability of such things as clubs and sports facilities in their neighbourhood, and the extent of school-based activities will be important. The ease with which they can travel to and from home, school or leisure centre may also be a factor.

The normal pattern of the teenagers' lives is structured around school during term-time and the interview focused on this part of the school year. Most arrived home having come straight from school. At some stage in the evening they did about an hour's homework. (This varied from under 2 hours a week to over 10 hours.) Two-thirds of the teenagers in the study said they belonged to a club or took part in an organized activity outside school hours. The most popular appeared to be sports clubs or teams of some kind, about half of which were associated with school. Youth clubs were the next most common activity mentioned, followed by uniformed organizations such as scouts and guides or music groups such as bands, orchestras or choirs. Taking part in one of these organized activities usually meant going out (or staying on at school) once or twice a week, and a number of the teenagers were involved with more than one.

Interests and hobbies

While not all of the teenagers in the survey were involved in such organized and supervised activities, almost all of them could name hobbies and interests which occupied part, if not all, of their spare time. The main interest among the boys was sport — predominantly team sports of some kind — followed by individual sports such as table tennis, badminton, swimming, weightlifting and cycling. Outdoor pastimes such as fishing, shooting or rabbiting, were the next most common group of interests, followed by using computers, making or listening to music, mending or building radios or motorcycles and cars, and indoor pursuits such as snooker, darts, cards, and boardgames. Among the girls some form of individual sport such as swimming, gymnastics, keep fit or badminton was the most popular pastime, followed by dancing or going to discos. Very few of them played team sports. They spent more time listening to music than boys and on indoor pastimes such as knitting, collecting, caring for pets, drawing and painting. Such differences in the interests of girls and boys will surprise few people, but it was evident that the girls were not as confined to home by their interests as might be thought. While the boys were clearly involved in more outdoor pursuits than the girls, girls were more likely than boys to mention organized indoor activities away from home such as discos or dancing lessons (Table 9).

Table 9
Location of main activities

	Boys (N = 362)	Girls (N = 355)
Outdoor	55%	33%
At home	33%	37%
Indoor away from home	3%	17%
Other, unclassified	9%	12%

Jobs and chores

Other calls on their spare time came from jobs, or from chores which they were expected to do at home. Studies of child-rearing practices among younger children and their families have often seen parental expectations about doing jobs around the house as an indication of good supervision and discipline (Newson and Newson, 1968; Wilson and Herbert, 1978) although it probably forms a minimal role in their lives (Medrich, 1982). Of the young teenagers in this study, around 70% — although rather more girls than boys — were expected to help in the house regularly, but were not usually paid for doing so. (Having such jobs to do was not in fact found to be related to other aspects of supervision or to delinquency among the teenagers in the study.) About one third of both boys and girls had a paid job apart from this, mostly paper rounds for the boys, the girls also babysitting or helping in a shop.

Going out

Apart from hobbies and organized activities, homework and household jobs, most of the teenagers went out during the week to see friends. It is this aspect of the lives of young teenagers — when they are most likely to be unsupervised and free of adult company — which causes most concern among parents and public. There are also indications from delinquency studies, (for instance, West and Farrington, 1977) that the extent to which a child goes out is related to getting into trouble. A study of 11–15 year-old boys in Liverpool, for example, found that those who spent three or more hours an evening hanging about the streets were more likely to admit to vandalism than those spending more time at home (Gladstone, 1978). Other studies have similarly seen the extent to which a child spends time playing out of the house as an indication of parental vigilance or supervision (West, 1969; Wilson, 1980).

While it is to be expected that teenagers rather more than younger children will spend time out of the home with their friends — and indeed that they should do so — there was evidence in the survey of wide variations in the extent to which this happens. This was true both among those of the same sex and between the sexes. Boys, for example, went out to see their friends considerably more often during the week than girls. While this is clearly likely to vary with the time of year, over half of them, according to their own account, went out at least five times a week and many of them most days after school, compared with a third of the girls (Table 10).

There was, moreover, a wide divergence of opinion between the parents and the teenagers as to how often they did go out as Table 11 indicates. Parents gave consistently lower estimates than their son or daughter.

While these differences may have resulted from different interpretations on the part of the two groups of respondents, it is likely that at least part of the

20

Table 10
Going out to see friends: frequency during normal term time (teenagers' account)

	Boys	Girls
Less than once a week	11%	19%
1–2 times a week	20%	29%
3–4 times a week	16%	18%
5 or more times a week	53%	34%

Table 11
Going out to see friends: frequency during normal term time (parents' account)

	Boys	Girls
Less than once a week	18%	29%
1–2 times a week	35%	32%
3–4 times a week	18%	20%
5 or more times a week	29%	19%

discrepancy reflects the fact that parents do not pay a great deal of attention to how often their teenager does in fact go out.

Other differences in the patterns of activity of the boys and girls were also evident. Boys were more likely to go out somewhere with a number of friends, rather than with just one or two, although about a quarter of both sexes usually went out with a group of four or more. The boys also seemed less willing to spend time in mixed company than girls. About 60% spent their spare time mostly in the company of others of the same sex, compared with 45% of the girls. Finally, when the girls did go out they were more likely than the boys to go to the home of a friend than to be out on the street or elsewhere. Having friends visiting their own homes was common among almost all the sample, with the girls having rather more visitors. Among just over half the families this took place once or twice a week or less.

Saturday activities

To provide an overall picture of the kinds of ways in which teenagers used their free time, they were asked to describe their activities for the previous Saturday in terms of what they did, where they were and with whom. On average both the boys and the girls spent just under half their Saturday at home, and about the same amount on activities out of the home. The remainder was spent at the home of friends. Apart from eating meals the most common activities mentioned by the boys were watching television, taking part in outside sports or pastimes, and shopping. Watching television appeared to account for almost a quarter of their waking day. For the girls too it took up more of their day than any other activity — although they watched significantly less than the boys. Otherwise they were most likely to be found shopping or listening to music. Overall, the boys' activities were mostly carried out with a member of their family or alone. The girls spent the majority of their Saturday with members of their family.

Such a summary ignores the enormous variety in the lives of the young people in the survey. Some led very active lives with sports practice and outings with friends or family, homework and hobbies. Others had difficulty in describing their day and appeared to spend the day doing little specific and often watching television for long stretches of time. One teenager, for example, got up at about 10.30am and watched television, got dressed and ate, then went out on his bike until tea at 5.30. Another half-hour on his bike was followed by two hours at the fair and a final three and a half watching television until after midnight. Even with so rough a measure of the teenagers' activities there was evidence of a relationship with their own reports of offending. Delinquents (see Chapter 4) were likely to spend more of their Saturday out of the home and with friends, and less time with their parents or other family members.

On the basis of this brief account of how the teenagers spent their free time after school and on a Saturday it was possible to build up a very rough picture of their lives. Overall many of the teenagers have fairly busy lives during term-time with quite a lot of their free time still spent at home with parents or in activities which are likely to be supervised in some way. But this still leaves considerable periods of time with no direct adult supervision. There will also be school holidays and other days out of school during some twelve weeks of the year, when there may be less provision of organized activities, and when parents may find it difficult to be constantly available. It is these periods which perhaps present the greatest test for the teenagers — and their parents.

Earning and spending

Few observers would deny that the spending power of young teenagers today is considerably greater than that of former generations (Nissel, 1982). It is this which in part has helped to give them a life-style distinct from that of their parents or younger brothers and sisters. To what extent do parents of 14 and 15 year-olds still maintain some control over sources of money and how it is spent?

Eighty per cent of the sample (and rather more girls than boys) were receiving pocket money from their parents, in most cases on a regular basis, but about half the sample also got extra spending money from them from time to time. Altogether those receiving pocket money got about £7 a month. For about a quarter of the sample there was also the occasional gift of money from relatives. Apart from this those who were paid for jobs they did at home earned from £4−6 a month, those with jobs elsewhere about £16 a month. On the whole only about 20% of the teenagers thought that it was *very* important to have plenty of money to spend, and few of them (19%) reported disagreements with their parents over spending their money. Over the past month they had spent it on an enormous range of goods and services. The boys had spent money — in order of priority — on snacks, sports equipment, magazines and books, records and music cassettes, playing on arcade machines, and on clothes, and shoes. The girls had bought clothes and shoes, magazines and books, snacks, records and cassettes, disco tickets and jewellery. Less frequent items for both were cinema tickets, video films, football tickets, computer software, haircuts and cigarettes.

Their spending habits reflected in a sense their age-group's preoccupation in terms of music and style (Murdock, 1979) but most of the teenagers did not feel themselves to be drawn too much in that direction. When asked a series of questions about issues which might be important to young teenagers, doing well at school was thought to be 'very important' by two-thirds, and looking neat and tidy by half of them. Having lots of money to spend, looking grown up, and dressing in the latest style were thought 'quite important', while 60% thought it was 'not important' to keep up with the latest chart records.

Attitudes to crime

As a measure of their attitude to crime the teenagers were also asked their views about shoplifting, an offence which is particularly common among this age group. One parent indeed labelled it 'the disease of this generation'. Three-quarters (76%) of the teenagers thought it was very serious to take something worth £10 from a shop, and an even higher proportion (86%) would feel very guilty if they had done so on impulse. Almost all (96%) thought their parents would be very upset about it if they found out (Table 12).

Family relations: being with parents

Relationships between teenagers and their parents would seem to play an important part in determining how they act when they are away from them (Hirschi, 1969). Their relationship may in part be determined by the amount of time which parents and teenagers spend together, although the quality of the relationship is also important — time spent quarrelling or arguing may be more damaging than constructive.

23

Table 12
What teenagers expected would happen if, on impulse, they pinched something worth £10 from a shop

	Boys	Girls
Think it would be "very serious"	75%	77%
Would feel "very guilty"	82%	92%
Expect their parents would be "very upset"	95%	98%
Expect it would make a difference to their friends	39%	58%
Expect they would be "very likely" to be caught	31%	43%
If caught, expect to end up facing a court	46%	53%

Despite the greater amounts of time which this age-group spend away from home compared with younger children, the survey suggests that there are clearly still numerous opportunities for them to be with their parents. This may be before and after school, during meal times, and in the evenings and at weekends. Such contact may involve chatting or discussing things with them, working at hobbies or jobs about the house, or going out or on trips together. The activity record discussed above gives some indication that at weekends at least, just under half of the teenagers' time was spent with parents and brothers and sisters. One American study showed that watching television with parents was the most common activity 11 year-olds shared with their parents (Medrich *et al.*, 1982). Watching television appeared to take up a sizeable proportion of time spent at home with parents in this study too, although it is difficult to know whether this helps to reinforce the relationship between the teenager and the parents or not.

Asked whether there were activities they particularly enjoyed doing or talking about with their parents, two-thirds of the boys felt they shared interests with their father, and a third with their mother. Just under half of the girls shared particular interests with their father or their mother. Another indication of the extent to which the two generations still held interests in common was how much the teenagers went out still with their families (see Table 13).

Overall 62% of the girls and slightly fewer (52%) boys went out *at least* once a week with their families. (This proved to be strongly related to other aspects of supervision and delinquent behaviour reported by the teenagers.)

Table 13
How often teenagers go out with their parents

	Boys	Girls
Twice or more a week	22%	34%
Once a week	30%	28%
Once a fortnight	16%	14%
Once a month	16%	13%
Less than once a month	16%	11%

Talking to parents

Talking forms a crucial part of family life. The early interviews conducted for the study illustrated the wide variations in the extent to which parents and teenagers talked together. Some parents spoke of their teenager as being rather quiet or self-contained, spending a lot of time in their room; others presented graphic accounts of very lively and talkative children and of noisy discussions among family members. Other teenagers were out for much of their free time. Around two-thirds of the teenagers spent considerable time chatting to their parents — mostly to their mother, but quite often to both parents, and three-quarters or more took problems to them about school, friends, future jobs or other matters. Again it was mainly the mother to whom they went with problems, although this may be because mothers were more likely to be around after school or at other times. It may also be because both the girls and the boys felt that they could talk to them more easily about such things — 90% of boys and girls felt their mothers understood their problems fairly or very well, although 82% of the boys and 72% of the girls felt so about their fathers.

Attachment to parents

A number of writers have in recent years pointed to the neglect of fathers in family studies, and one group in particular has looked at the role of fathers in the lives of teenagers (Lewis, Newson and Newson, 1982). They suggest that boys who have poor relationships with their fathers are more likely to be delinquent and to do poorly at school than others. Two studies of probationers living at home and in probation hostels have similarly found a strong association between the quality of relationship between boys and their fathers or hostel wardens and the prevention of subsequent delinquency (Davies and Sinclair, 1971). In particular, boys with fathers or wardens who were judged to be firm but affectionate or kindly in their handling of their sons or residents were more successful in avoiding subsequent offending than others.

Having interests in common with their fathers, and feeling close to them were

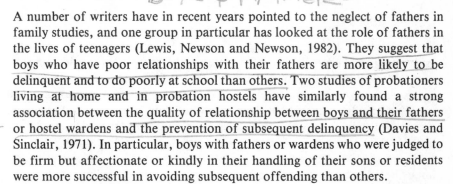

found to be important in this study too as Chapter 4 will show. Both teenagers and their parents were asked how close they felt to each other, and both gave almost identical accounts. About 62% of the boys and the girls felt they were very close to their mother, and about 46% very close to their father (see Table 14).

[handwritten annotation: Reported feeling close to mother]

Table 14
Closeness between teenagers and their parents

	Teenagers' account	
	Boys	Girls
Very close to mother	61% (n = 370)	63% (n = 363)
Very close to father	48% (n = 344)	42% (n = 332)
	Parents' account	
	Mothers	Husbands
Very close to son	58% (n = 378)	43% (n = 336)
Very close to daughter	63% (n = 373)	42% (n = 332)

Closeness between teenagers and their parents

It is difficult to know what 'closeness' means to individual people, yet there seemed to be a congruence of beliefs between parents and teenagers in the survey about how close they were. Overall there still seemed to be a strong sense of the family belonging together as a whole.

Parental strictness

Most of the teenagers did not regard their parents' approach to their activities as too strict, and generally accepted that they still had a right to tell them what to do. While it was a common complaint that their friends were allowed to do things they were not, two-thirds (64%) of the boys and girls thought their parents were about average in their control of their behaviour and activities. Only 18% thought them *too* strict. Surprisingly, parents themselves were more likely to think themselves stricter than average — over 27% thought so. It was evident too that the teenagers — like their parents — did not see them imposing rules; rather they felt that they had 'understandings' about what they were allowed to do. Making rules was only necessary 'when things went wrong'. It also seemed important to the teenagers that their parents held strong views about what they were allowed to do. A parent (or indeed a teacher) who did not impose some sense of discipline and structure on their lives was not thought to care about them. Caring, in fact, seemed an important concept for these teenagers. Most of the sample reported that their parents had strong views about a number of issues. These included what time they should be home at night and — for the girls — where they were allowed to go. Parents were also reported to have strong views about how the boys spent their money and how they should dress. Parents seemed less often concerned with the sorts of friends the teenagers could have, or the kinds of things they could do with their friends. There were, predictably therefore, some variations in parental concern about the activities and behaviour of girls and boys in the sample (Table 15).

Table 15
Parents' views: % with strong views about...

	Boys	Girls
the time you should be home at night	75%	85%
where you are allowed to go	45%	71%
how you spend your money	67%	48%
the sorts of friends you can have	41%	42%
the sorts of things you can do with them	44%	49%
the way you should dress	67%	36%

Gender difference

What is apparent from this Table, as the previous chapter has outlined, is the greater degree of supervision exercised by parents over the lives of the girls in terms of their activities away from home — parents exercised stricter control over where they were allowed to go and when they should come home at night (Smart and Smart, 1978).

A survey such as the present one which is only concerned with one point in time cannot measure how far relationships within the family or the extent of control exercised by parents may have changed from one generation to another. A recent American study has attempted to trace changes between generations by asking groups of people of different ages to describe how they spent their free time at the age of 17 (Felson and Gottfredson, 1984). While such methods have their problems, the research suggested that there have been major shifts in young American teenagers' lives in terms of how much time they spend at home at weekends, how late they stay out, whether the family eats meals together, and how much of their time is spent with their parents or adult relatives. Time spent with parents or adults has decreased, that with adolescents or at least away from adult contact has increased. Such changes may well mean that parents and adults have less opportunities to supervise their teenagers in terms of direct surveillance or control.

The current survey can provide no evidence of similar changes in this country, although it is probable that they have also occurred here over the past twenty years or more. The findings described in this chapter suggest that at 14 and 15, teenagers do still have considerable contact with their parents while the parents have considerable opportunities to influence their activities and behaviour. Both contact and influence appear to be greater in the case of girls than boys. The next chapter is concerned with examining the relationship between such supervision exercised by parents and delinquency.

4 Parental supervision and how it relates to delinquency

The previous two chapters have provided a wide-ranging account of the survey's findings about teenagers and their parents. The present chapter looks more closely at the direct influence of supervision on delinquency.

Defining parental supervision and delinquency

Parental supervision

In one sense, almost any aspect of parents' attempts to control children's behaviour can be regarded as supervision. Rules about watching television, washing up or helping around the house, doing homework, wearing particular clothes etc. are all different aspects of parental control. But because juvenile offending usually takes place when teenagers are away from home and with their friends, the present study focuses on supervision in relation to teenagers' behaviour in these situations. And because at 14 and 15 direct supervision — in the form of surveillance or chaperonage — is usually inappropriate outside the home, the study uses a definition of indirect supervision based on parents' knowledge about their children's activities when they are out with their friends. This is consistent with the broad theme of approaches to parental supervision contained in earlier research (eg Hirschi, 1969; Wilson, 1980).

Supervision was measured in terms of how often parents knew who their son or daughter was with, where they were going and what they were doing. Those who responded "almost always" to *all* three questions were regarded, for the purpose of analysis, as exerting "high" supervision, those who did not respond in this way were defined as providing "low" supervision. (The relationship between a number of other possible measures of supervision and delinquency is examined in Appendix 2. But this additional analysis provides no basis for improving a definition based on the three items: who, where and what.)

Delinquency

Previous studies both in this country and elsewhere, discussed earlier in Chapter 1, have shown that many teenage children admit having done something which could have got them into trouble with the police (see, for example, Shapland, 1978; Belson, 1975; Campbell, 1981; Gladstone, 1978; Hindelang, Hirschi and Weiss, 1981; West and Farrington, 1973). Although offending is at its peak during these teenage years, comparatively few young people of 14 or 15 have a police record (about one in twelve males and one in fifty females will have been convicted by their sixteenth birthday and similar numbers cautioned) and official statistics inevitably present an incomplete picture of the overall incidence of offending. This study, however, is concerned not only with young people who have been in trouble with the police or the courts but with the much larger group whose present conduct raises the possibility that this might happen.

This group was identified on the basis of teenagers' responses[1] to a series of questions about a standard set of offences. Briefly, teenagers were asked to sort a set of 21 cards describing various illegal acts — such as breaking windows and shoplifting — (see Appendix 3) into two groups: those they had ever carried out and those they had not. Then they were asked whether in the previous 12 months they had committed any of the behaviours in the first group, and, if they had, how often they had done so.

Those who reported carrying out one or more offences from the standard set of illegal acts in the year preceding the interview were defined as 'delinquent', the others were defined as 'non-delinquent'. Consideration was, however, given to an alternative definition of delinquency in terms of having committed five or more delinquent acts in the previous 12 months. The results based on this measure of more serious involvement in delinquency are presented in Appendix 2, but briefly they are broadly similar to those based on the main definition and which will be detailed later in this chapter.

How much delinquency?

Just under a half (43%) of the teenagers in the survey reported having committed at least one illegal act in the 12 months prior to the survey (see Table 16). The prevalence of delinquency is higher for boys than for girls (at 49% and 39% respectively) but the difference is much smaller than might be expected from Criminal Statistics (see Fig. 1). The higher overall ratio of male to female offenders is, however, consistent with the main body of evidence

---

[1] Despite the now widespread use of admissions of offending to classify individuals in terms of delinquency, the method is not without its critics (see, for example, Walker 1983). Early delinquency research relied on official records, primarily of convictions, to identify offenders. However, subsequent studies using the self-report method have revealed the incomplete nature of official statistics on offenders. For many forms of anti-social and illegal behaviour, those who had never committed the act were, particularly in the case of boys, clearly in the minority. The critics of self-report measures of delinquency counsel against accepting the results at face value since for many of the behaviours about which individuals are questioned there are no reliable means of validating the answers given. Proponents of the method, however, point out that where cross-checking has been possible, then the reliability of the responses has been reasonably high, similarly, consistency in responding has been used as an indicator of truthfulness (see, for example, Hindelang, Hirschi and Weis, 1981). Moreover, when discrepancies have occurred the tendency — at least in studies in this country — has been in the direction of concealment rather than exaggeration. None of this is to deny that the self-report method is imperfect. The advantages of this measure of offending, however, over the present alternatives appear sufficiently great to warrant its use.

based on self-report studies (Hindelang, 1971; Campbell, 1981). As in previous surveys of teenage offending, the most commonly admitted offences involved theft or dishonesty (eg shoplifting, stealing from the family, fare evasion) and vandalism (eg smashing bottles in the street, damaging school property)[2]. The types of delinquency committed by boys and girls were remarkably similar. As Table 17 shows, for both groups the three most frequent bases for inclusion in the delinquency category were involvement in theft only, in both theft and vandalism and in vandalism only. Appendix 3 gives a fuller account of the numbers of teenagers admitting committing each delinquent act in the preceding year.

Table 16
Offending in the past 12 months

	Number of delinquent acts		
	0	*1–4*	*5 or more*
Boys (N = 378)	194 (51%)	106 (28%)	78 (21%)
Girls (N = 373)	227 (61%)	82 (22%)	64 (17%)

Table 17
Types of delinquency in past 12 months

Numbers admitting to	Boys	Girls
Theft only	46	44
Theft + vandalism	46	41
Vandalism only	34	29
Theft + vandalism + other	30	13
Other only	11	7
Theft + other	9	4
Vandalism + other	8	8
Admitted none of these	194	227

[2] Direct comparisons between the results of the present and previous surveys are difficult. Variations in the method and design of research and in the recency and nature of the samples studied are likely to distort the nature of any differences which may exist. In adition, real changes may occur in the prevalence of delinquent behaviour over time. The most similar survey to the present enquiry formed part of the recent British Crime Survey (BCS) (Hough and Mayhew, 1983). This contained a component on self-reported offending and the frequency with which parallel offences were admitted was roughly comparable for 16-year-old respondents in the BCS, although in both this and the present survey the incidence of offending was somewhat lower than other — but less recent or representative — research has indicated.

Does parental supervision influence delinquency?

Using these measures of supervision and delinquency, Table 18 shows that delinquency was less common among teenagers experiencing high supervision than among those subject to low supervision.

Table 18

Percentage delinquent at two levels of parental supervision

	High Supervision	Low Supervision
Boys		
$X^2 = 7.9$, 1 d.f., p< .005	41%	56%
	(N = 179)	(N = 199)
Girls		
$X^2 = 24.9$, 1 d.f., p< .001	29%	55%
	(N = 224)	(N = 149)

Moreover, as Table 18 also shows, teenage boys were much more likely to receive low supervision than teenage girls ($X^2 = 11.4$, 1 d.f., p< .001). And under low supervision teenage girls were as likely as boys to be delinquent, while under high supervision the greater involvement of boys in offending was clearly marked. Because the effects of supervision on delinquency are likely to be different for boys and girls, the remainder of the analyses consider these two groups separately.

Clearly, the existence of a relationship between supervision and delinquency does not enable us to conclude that this is the most important or the only factor involved in teenage offending. And the remainder of the present chapter is concerned with testing how far supervision is important in comparison with other family and individual factors.

I. Delinquency: boys

Not only was there a clear relationship between supervision and recent offending, there were, as was expected, a considerable number of other ways in which delinquent boys differed from their non-delinquent counterparts. Details of these are presented in full in Appendix 4, but are summarised briefly below under five main headings. (Part B of Appendix 4 contains a description of the survey measures on which delinquent and non-delinquent teenagers did not differ.)

i. Family differences

The findings suggest that boys who admitted offending in the 12 months prior to the survey had a rather different kind of relationship with their

32

family than those who said they had not broken the law during this period. It appears that delinquent teenagers were less willing to accept parental control over the way they spent their time out of the home with their friends. In addition, delinquent teenagers often seem to have some difficulty in their relationship with their fathers.[3] In particular, delinquent teenagers were less close to their fathers and less often felt that their fathers understood their problems. There was no evidence that parents of boys who had offended were any less concerned about what they got up to when they were out of the home. On the contrary, parents of delinquents were more likely to worry about how they spent their time with their friends and more often had rows with their sons about this.

ii. School differences

Among delinquent boys antipathy towards school was not difficult to detect. Success at school was a less frequently desired, or attained, goal. Delinquent teenagers less often took their work at school or their homework seriously and they less often felt that doing well at school was important. They more often played truant and less often felt that they were doing well at school.

iii. Friends/going out differences

The survey showed that delinquent boys spent more time with their friends, generally away from both their own and their friends' homes. Delinquents were more often involved with girls, either as girlfriends or as members of mixed groups. In addition, the values and past behaviour of their friends were more likely to provide a context in which the constraints against offending were likely to be weaker. Their friends, for example, were more likely to include those who had themselves committed offences and to whom it would make little or no difference if, for example, the boys stole.

iv. Differences in beliefs

Boys who had committed offences in the last year appeared to have rather different ideas about the implications of lawbreaking. Their answers to a series of questions about a hypothetical shoplifting incident (see Table 12) implied that delinquents regarded the act in a less serious light and less frequently said they would expect unpleasant consequences to follow. Delinquents less often expected to feel guilty if they stole. In addition, they were less likely to expect to be caught if they did steal and were less likely to expect that being convicted of stealing would make a difference either to their friends or at school.

---

[3] Chapter 6 includes a detailed discussion of the relationship between delinquency and family characteristics in one-parent households.

v. Police contact differences

Delinquents more frequently reported involvement with the police. This included seeking assistance as well as being stopped on the street and questioned. Moreover, boys who had offended were less likely to say that the police in their area treated young people fairly.

As we have seen, the survey identified a large number of differences between delinquents and non-delinquents and it is possible that some of these are more closely implicated in teenagers' delinquency than is supervision. The contribution of parental supervision to differences in offending among teenage boys was assessed using logistic regression analysis — a technique which allows the independent effects of supervision on delinquency to be estimated (and this form of analysis is used throughout the report). The ten variables, apart from parental supervision, which were included in this first analysis were those which were strongly associated with delinquency ($p < .001$) and which had, at least in principle, some implications for how delinquency could be tackled.

The analysis indicated that four of the factors examined could explain a significant amount of the variation in delinquency among boys in this age-group (G-square reduced from 450.3 with 324 d.f. to 334.4 with 320 d.f.)[4]. This showed that:

Boys who reported their friends were relatively more involved in delinquency were almost eight (7.7) times as likely to be delinquent.

Boys who said they would not feel "very guilty" if they stole were about five (4.7) times as likely to be delinquent.

Boys who said they were closer to their mothers, rather than to their fathers or equally close to both, were almost three (2.9) times as likely to be delinquent.

Boys who usually went out three or more times a week to see their friends were about twice (1.8 times) as likely to be delinquent.

Counting each of these four attributes as an 'adverse factor' provides a possible score ranging from 0 to 4. Table 19 below shows that as the adverse factor score increases so does the proportion of boys who are delinquent and for those with the highest scores over 80% are delinquent.

[4] The fit of the model was significantly improved (G-square reduced from 333.4 with 320 d.f. to 329.2 with 319 d.f.) by adding in, as a fifth factor, an interaction term representing the joint effects of teenagers' accounts of which parent they felt closest to and of how often they went out during the week to see their friends. The likelihood of delinquency among boys who said they were either equally close to both parents or closer to their father *and* who normally went out three or more times a week was lower than would be expected on the basis of the separate effects of each of these two factors.

34

Table 19
Boys: relationship between adverse factor score and delinquency

Number of adverse factors	N	Proportion delinquent
0 or 1	84	23%
2	136	49%
3	77	64%
4	28	80%

Taking these four separate factors into account, however, reduced the association between the parental supervision index and delinquency for teenage boys to chance levels. That is, after allowing for those factors, parental supervision appeared to have no direct or independent effect on delinquency. Examination of the relationship between these four measures and parental supervision showed that it was primarily the link between supervision and friends' delinquency which accounted for the apparent association between supervision and teenagers' delinquency. Differences in supervision were unrelated to teenage offending after taking account of friends' involvement in delinquency. Thus, among those with delinquent friends those who were poorly supervised were not more likely to be delinquent than boys who were well supervised. The implications of this conclusion and other results presented in this and the following chapter are discussed more fully in Chapter 7.

II. Delinquency: girls

As in the case of teenage boys, differences between delinquent and non-delinquent girls were not confined to the variations in parental supervision shown in Table 18. These results are presented in full in Appendix 4, but are summarised below.

i. Family differences

The overall impression from the survey is that in their relationships with their families, delinquent girls appeared to be more remote from both their parents but especially their fathers. This is particularly evident in terms of closeness, involvement and communication. Moreover, delinquent girls were more frequently involved in rows with their parents over not only their appearance but also how they spent their time with their friends. Especially frequent were rows about the time they came home at night. Girls who admitted committing offences were also less willing to tell their parents about how they spent their time with their friends and had parents who were more likely to worry about what they got up to with their friends.

ii. School differences

The survey results indicate that for delinquent girls, school was less likely to play a significant part in their lives and these girls appeared to be less interested in the rewards offered by success at school. Delinquent teenagers more often disliked school and less often took their work at school or their homework seriously. They more often played truant and less often felt that doing well at school was important.

iii. Friends/going out differences

Girls who had offended in the previous 12 months were more likely to spend time away from home in the company of their friends and these were more likely to include boys. In addition, friends of delinquent girls were more likely to have committed offences themselves and were more likely to include boyfriends.

iv. Differences in beliefs

The findings of the survey are consistent with the idea that delinquent girls tended to view the implications of breaking the law in rather a different light to those who had not offended. Expectations of unpleasant consequences following a hypothetical shoplifting incident were consistently less frequent. Delinquent girls not only less often thought that stealing was a serious offence or that they would feel guilty if they stole but they were less likely to expect to be caught and less often expected to be upset by the sentence they would receive if they were convicted.

v. Police contact differences

Involvement with the police both as a source of assistance and in their investigative role was higher for girls who had committed offences in the previous year. Delinquent girls were more likely to have been stopped on the street and questioned by the police and to feel that the police locally treated young people unfairly. However, they were also more likely to have asked for help and to have reported crimes and other problems.

The influence of parental supervision, independent of its association with other factors related to delinquency among teenage girls, was again assessed and just six out of the eighteen factors examined accounted for a substantial and significant amount of the variation in delinquency among girls (G-square reduced from 430.2 with 323 d.f. to 294.3 with 317 d.f.)[5]. This showed that:

---

[5] The ability of the analysis to account for the variation in delinquency among girls was significantly improved (G-square reduced from 294.3 with 317 d.f. to 290.4 with 316 d.f.) by adding in as a seventh factor an interaction term representing the joint effect of girls' feelings about how well their father understands their problems and their attitude to their work at school. The likelihood of delinquency among girls who felt that their fathers did not understand their problems *and* who did not take their work at school very seriously was lower than would be expected on the basis of the separate effects of these two factors on the probability of delinquency.

36

Girls who reported their friends were relatively more involved in delinquency were about fifteen (14.8) times as likely to be delinquent.

Girls whose parents did not almost always know who their daughters were with, or where they were or what they were doing were about four (3.7) times as likely to be delinquent.

Girls who felt that their fathers did not understand their problems very well were about twice (2.5 times) as likely to be delinquent.

Girls who felt that stealing was not "very serious" were about twice (2.3 times) as likely to be delinquent.

Girls who said their attitude to their work at school was not "very serious" were about twice (2.2 times) as likely to be delinquent.

Girls who thought it would make little difference to their friends if they stole were about twice (1.8 times) as likely to be delinquent.

Table 20 shows the relationship between these adverse factors and delinquency. For girls with the highest scores all were delinquent.

Table 20
Girls: relationship between adverse factor score and delinquency

Number of adverse factors	N	Proportion delinquent
0	12	0%
1	73	16%
2	107	26%
3	79	56%
4	41	66%
5 or 6	12	100%

Summary of delinquency analysis

While the survey results indicated that the independent effects of parental supervision were markedly different between boys and girls, there was a high degree of similarity in the other significant factors identified by the analyses. Three of the characteristics identified as important in their association with delinquency among teenage boys had their parallel in the analysis of the girls' data. For both boys and girls it made a significant difference to their chances of being delinquent whether their friends were delinquent, what their views were about stealing, and what their feelings were towards their father.

Among boys, the analysis showed that once account was taken of the kind of

37

friends the teenagers had, then parental knowledge of the details of how they spend their spare time was unrelated to the chances of their being delinquent. For girls, however, differences in parental supervision were related to delinquency in these teenage years even after allowing for the effects of all the other influences on offending identified by the analysis. This suggests that, over and above whatever influence friends exert, parents who know in detail about how spare time is spent with friends less often have delinquent daughters.

As was shown in Table 18 at the beginning of the present chapter, girls were much less likely to receive low supervision than boys and Chapter 3 (Table 9) shows that parents are likely to have different ideas about the appropriate level of supervision for their sons and daughters. This suggests that low supervision has rather different implications for boys than for girls. For teenage girls it seems more likely that low supervision is indicative of a less prominent or intrusive role played by parents in the lives of their children (see also, Campbell, 1981).

5 What explains differences in parental supervision?

We have seen that parental supervision independently explains rather less of the variation in teenage offending for the 14–15 age-group than might have been expected and none in the case of boys' delinquency. Alternative forms of analysis, however, might well have reached different conclusions. The results of the analysis of boys' delinquency, for example, suggest that supervision exercised by parents would have appeared a more significant influence on delinquency had no account been taken of teenagers' friends (see, for example, Thornton and James, 1979; Rutter and Giller, 1983 (Chapter 8)). One important aim of the study — to isolate the contribution of supervision to the prevention of delinquency — meant that friends' delinquency needed to be seen as part of the background against which possible changes in parents' roles could be assessed.Differences in supervision were, however, consistently related to a broad range of factors which form a useful basis for interpreting how parent-child relationships influence supervision levels[1]. These correlates of differences in parental supervision are detailed in Appendix 6, but are outlined, briefly, below.

Boys

Among teenage boys poor or low supervision was associated with a reluctance to tell their parents about how they spend their time with their friends and with being less likely to chat with both their parents. Moreover — contrary to what might have been expected — parents who tended to worry about what their sons were up to when they were out with their friends, or who did not feel that they could trust their sons to behave, or who had a poor view of their neighbourhood were more likely to exert low supervision. And boys who were poorly supervised were more likely to go out to see their friends at least three times a week, to meet their friends in groups of four or more, to be unreliable about coming home at the agreed time and to have been stopped on the street and questioned by the police.

A significant amount of the differences in parental supervision among boys could be accounted for by six variables[2] (G-square reduced from 511.6 with 369 d.f to 393.8 with 363 d.f.).

---

[1] To emphasise factors with relatively strong relationships with parental supervision, only those with Chi-square values significant at least at the .001 level are referred to. A full account of all statistically significant factors is presented in Appendix 6.

[2] The ability of the analysis to account for the variation in parental supervision among teenage boys was significantly increased by including as a seventh factor an interaction term representing the joint effects on supervision of the frequency with which the teenager went to see his

The analysis showed that:

teenage boys who were unwilling to tell their parents about how they spend their time with their friends were about five (5.2) times more likely to be in the low supervision group

— teenage boys who were less often trusted by their parents to behave themselves when out with their friends were about three (2.7) times more likely to be in the low supervision group

— teenage boys who went out three or more times a week to see their friends were about three (2.6) times more likely to be in the low supervision group

— teenage boys whose parents had a poor view of their neighbourhood were about twice (2.2 times) as likely to be in the low supervision group

— teenage boys who relatively often had rows with their parents over how they spent their time with their friends were about twice (1.8 times) as likely to be in the low supervision group

— teenage boys who were unreliable about coming home at what their parents called a sensible time were about twice (1.7 times) as likely to be in the low supervision group

The survey gives little indication that variations in supervision reflect parents' concern to "safeguard" their sons. Supervision in fact tended to be lower for teenagers whose parents did not feel that they could trust their sons and for sons who lived in neighbourhoods regarded in a relatively poor light by their parents. What does seem to be important in understanding why parents differ in how well-informed they are about what their sons are doing when they are out with their friends is the parent-child relationship itself. It seems reasonable to suppose that some teenagers more than others resent not only being asked about how they spend their spare time, but also anything more than a minimal degree of interest from parents about their life outside the home. Being reticent about these details, being unreliable about coming home, and having rows about going out to see their friends are strong indicators that variations in parental supervision among boys more often reflect their own ideas about what supervision should be than their parents' ideas. Those who are subject to weak supervision appear to be considerably less willing to accept parents' views of what their supervisory role should be.

Just as not all children are equally willing to accept control parents vary in their enthusiasm to impose it. Some are more willing than others to tolerate

---

friends and whether the boy had rows with his parents about his going out (G-square was reduced from 393.8 with 363 d.f. to 380.6 with 362 d.f.). This indicated that teenagers who went out more than average *and* who had rows with their parents about going out were more likely to be poorly supervised than would be expected on the basis of the separate effects of these two factors on supervision.

their children's independence and while the survey indicates that at 14 and 15 low parental supervision is closely associated with factors relating to teenagers' willingness to accept parental control, there is no compelling reason to interpret this as a 'failure' of parenting.

Girls

Among girls poor or low supervision was associated not only with offending but also with a number of other differences in family relationships, in particular with girls being unwilling to tell their parents about how they spend their time with their friends or being less willing to discuss their problems or difficulties with their parents and being less likely to go out with their families. In addition, parents who exerted low supervision were less likely to expect that their daughters would stay out of trouble with the police over the next few years and more likely to think it unfair for parents to be made responsible for fines imposed on their children and to have a relatively poor view of their neighbourhood.

Also highly significantly associated with differences in supervision were housing tenure and the age at which mothers left school. Girls who lived in rented property or whose mothers left school at 15 or earlier were more likely to be poorly supervised. Moreover, low supervision was associated with girls who often went out to see their friends or who often had friends to their home, with parents who worried what their daughters were up to with their friends or who were less likely to trust their daughters to behave themselves when out, with daughters who had rows with their parents about going out or who were less reliable about coming home at what their parents called a sensible time or who had rows with their parents about the time they should be home.

In addition, girls who were interested in boyfriends were more likely to be poorly supervised. Poorly supervised girls were also more likely to have been stopped on the street and questioned by the police. In relation to school factors, low supervision was related to disliking school and playing truant. Similarly, girls subject to low supervision were more likely to have parents who expected them to leave at 16 and more likely to feel that doing well at school was unimportant.

The analysis identified the factors most strongly related to variations in parental supervision among teenage girls. Seven variables[3] were independently associated with differences in supervision and accounted for a significant

---

[3] Adding in as an eighth factor to the analysis an interaction term based on the joint effect of whether the girls were prepared to share their problems with their parents and whether they had rows about the time they should be home at night improved the ability of the model to account for the variation in supervision among teenage girls (G-square was reduced from 307.7 with 349 d.f. to 303.7 with 348 d.f.). This indicated that girls who tended not to share their problems *and* who had rows about the time they should be home at night were less likely to be poorly supervised than the separate effects of these two factors would imply.

proportion of the overall variation in parental supervision (G-square was reduced from 480.7 with 356 d.f. to 307.7 with 349 d.f.) and:

— teenage girls who were unwilling to tell their parents about how they spend their time with their friends were about six (5.8) times more likely to be in the low supervision group

— teenage girls who went out three or more times a week to see their friends were about five (4.9) times more likely to be in the low supervision group

— teenage girls whose mothers left school at or before 15 were about four (4.5) times more likely to be in the low supervision group

— teenage girls who tended not to share their problems with their parents were about three (2.9) times more likely to be in the low supervision group

— teenage girls who were unreliable about coming home at a "sensible" time were about three (2.7) times more likely to be in the low supervision group

— teenage girls who were delinquent were about twice (2.2 times) as likely to be in the low supervision group

— teenage girls who had rows with their parents about the time they should come home at night were twice as likely to be in the low supervision group

As was the case with teenage boys, the dominant factors associated with supervision seem to indicate that girls who are poorly supervised are seeking a measure of independence which exceeds what their parents are prepared to concede. Related to this is an apparent distancing of the girl from her parents in that poorly supervised girls are less likely to be open with their parents either about their own problems or about how they spend their time with their friends. In addition, there is a strong indication that girls who are poorly supervised have strong interests outside the family home: they are more often out with friends, they are unreliable about and have rows with their parents about coming home. The association between the age at which mothers left school and parental supervision might well indicate differences in attitudes to the upbringing of girls but no direct evidence is available from the survey.

Summary of supervision analyses

While the overlap between the factors identified as important in understanding the variation in supervision of boys and girls was not as great as it was for delinquency, there were again three which were common to both groups of teenagers. These were: teenagers' willingness to give their parents information about their activities with their friends, whether teenagers went out three or more times a week and whether teenagers were reliable about coming home at "sensible" times in the evenings. For both boys and girls the first of these was the factor most strongly associated with differences in supervision.

The purpose of analysing the data to examine the correlates of supervision was to clarify the implications of the study's definition of parental supervision. This showed that it was possible to characterise the factors related to low supervision for both boys and girls. The indication is that despite parents' wishes to be informed about what their teenagers are up to when they are out with their friends, whether they are well-informed or not depends very much on the teenagers themselves. Those who are less involved with their families appear to be less prepared to share their lives outside the home with them. For boys the quality of their relationships with their families did not appear particularly important in its association with delinquency for the 14–15 age-group. For girls, however, the opposite seemed to be the case. Girls who are relatively distant from their families tend to be both poorly supervised and involved in delinquency.

6 Delinquency and supervision: one-parent families

In the analysis of teenage offending reported in Chapter 4, delinquency in boys was found to be closely associated with their responses to a question about whether they felt closer to their mother or their father, and girls' delinquency was related to responses to an item about how well they felt their father understood their problems. As a result, data from families with information missing from certain sections of the questionnaire were not included. Specifically, boys without both parents in the household and from girls where the father was missing from the household were excluded from the analysis. Inevitably, this meant that one-parent families were under-represented.

There is, however, little doubt that the proportion of children not living with both their natural parents is increasing (see, for example, Finer Report, 1974; Rimmer, 1981; Jackson, 1982). The second of these reports, for example, suggests that as many as one in eight children are presently living in families headed by one parent, and just 80% of children aged 10–15 are living with both natural parents. On the same basis, it has been estimated that 1.6 million children will have the families of which they are part disrupted by divorce over the next 10 years.

One-parent family status is, however, not inevitably a permanent one. Families presently headed by a lone parent may, at some future date, as "re-marriage" becomes increasingly frequent, become a two-parent family again. Similarly, it is likely that many of the families regarded by the survey as intact will, at an earlier stage, have been disrupted by the loss of one of the partners.

In the present survey 18 of the 751 teenagers (2.4%) were living with a lone father and 75 (10%) with a lone mother. Moreover, of the 658 teenagers living in a two-parent family, 91% (602/658) were living with both their natural parents. While the figure for families headed by lone fathers is slightly higher than might be expected (see, for example, Rimmer, 1981), that for children living with both biological parents is identical to that indicated by OPCS for the 10–15 age group in 1979 (Population Trends 18, Table 1).

Early ideas about the causes of delinquency (see, for example, Glueck and Glueck, 1950), often based on studies of convicted juveniles, implicated "broken homes" as an important agent in the production of delinquency (for a review, see Rankin, 1983). Later research which has taken account of causes of break-up and the age of the children has confirmed an association between homes broken by marital disruption and offending (Wadsworth, 1979; West, 1982). The present study, however, while not distinguishing between one-parent families, found that the prevalence of delinquency was *not* higher among teenagers from one-parent households (Gladstone, 1978) reports a similar finding for vandalism). Furthermore, the scores for teenagers on those measures identified as most closely related to delinquency (see Chapter 4) were not significantly different for boys living in one-parent households. This was also the case for girls with the exception of parental supervision, with girls from one-parent families being more likely to receive low supervision.

There is, however, still the question of whether children from families headed by a lone parent differ in other ways from children living with both parents. Data were examined for a wide range of other family and individual characteristics which might be thought to be influenced by single-parent status. The survey, however, indicates that there were no differences in feelings of closeness between lone parents and their children, in the extent to which they shared an interest or hobby, in how often they had rows about the teenager going out, in whether they had delinquent friends, in how often their parents fixed a time for them to be home, or what that time was, in whether they were trusted to behave themselves when out with their friends, how often they had been stopped by the police and questioned, in how willing teenagers were to tell their parents about how they spent their time with friends, in whether they were more seriously involved in delinquency, in whether they met their friends in groups. In contrast, there was an association for both boys and girls between single-parent family status and tenure type with single-parent households being significantly more likely to live in rented property. In addition, girls from single-parent families were more likely to go out to see their friends three or more times a week, to have a paid job at weekends and to live in neighbourhoods regarded unfavourably by their parent.

Summary: one-parent families

The notion that one-parent families are, in any general sense, "criminogenic" receives no support from the results of the present survey. Not only were there no differences in the prevalence of delinquency but also largely absent were differences in factors which might be causally related to delinquency. This suggests it may be unwise to assume that more one-parent families must mean more delinquency or that they are *necessarily* more lax in their supervision or less able to provide support or affection than two-parent families. Clearly, life in single-parent families is often more difficult but no less caring (Jackson, 1982).

Family stress: delinquency and supervision

While early research concerned itself with the structural aspects of family functioning (such as the effects of parental absence), more recent work, for example, by Wilson (1991) has emphasised stress (the result of low income, overcrowding, poor housing etc.) in the causation of delinquency. This to some degree represents an attempt to make more explicit the economic and social context in which family life takes place. There seems little doubt that the circumstances of families at the margin of existence, whose living conditions are poor and whose prospects are bleak are unlikely to allow parents the patience, endurance or understanding which they often require in their relations with their teenage children. The present survey was designed to provide a representative picture of family life across the country as a whole and is not, therefore, ideally suited to looking at how extremes of stress on families influences the chances of delinquency among children.

Nevertheless, it seemed worthwhile to examine data which might usefully indicate families with particular economic and/or social difficulties. To this end an index of family stress was constructed based on four measures, these were:

a. whether the family was headed by a lone parent *or* whether the father was unemployed *or* whether the family was in social class groups IV or V (based on the father's job)

b. whether there were 4 or more children living in the family

c. whether parents felt their neighbourhood was not a good one in which to raise children

d. whether the family lived in rented accommodation

Family stress and delinquency

The absence of any clear relationship between family stress (at least as represented by the index constructed for the analysis) and delinquency holds for boys and girls, although only the aggregated data are presented in Table 21. The results are essentially unchanged when stress is examined in relation to

Table 21
Delinquency, supervision and family stress

"Stress" score	0	1	2	3 + 4
Percentage with delinquent teenager	41	49	41	49
Percentage exerting low supervision	37	52	56	59
Number of families	353	199	136	63

46

those more seriously involved in delinquency (ie those who report having committed five or more delinquent acts in the 12 months preceding the survey). A major difficulty in looking at the relationship between family stress and delinquency was that almost none of the candidate measures obtained in the survey was closely related to delinquency.

Family stress and supervision

The effects of stress on family functioning might be expected to extend beyond delinquency to other aspects of the parent-child relationship. Indeed, one of the ways in which stress might be hypothesised to increase the chances of delinquency is through parents' ability or interest in supervising their children. Using the same definition of family stress as in the previous section, there was found to be a significant relationship with parental supervision. For both boys and girls, families with high scores on family stress were more likely to exert low levels of supervision. As Table 21 shows, the presence of a single "adverse" factor is sufficient to increase the likelihood of poor supervision, and stress scores from 1 to 4 carry almost the same risk of poor supervision.

Whether family stress is an important *direct* influence on parental supervision at this age is, however, in some doubt. The preceding chapter showed that the main influences on supervision levels more closely reflected interaction between parents and their teenagers. Instead, the effects of family stress may be important in determining the past and present development of relationships between children and their parents.

7 What can parents do?

The preceding chapters of this report have given an overall picture of the lives of the teenagers and their parents in relation to supervision and delinquency. This suggests that parents were still exercising supervision over their young teenagers in a number of ways, and that the teenagers on the whole accepted that their parents should do so but there were clearly differences in the supervision exercised over boys and girls. There was still a considerable amount of contact between family members and of opportunities for parents to influence teenagers' activities and behaviour. Parents, perhaps not surprisingly, were not as well informed about the activities of their teenagers as they thought.

Chapters 4 and 5, however, have shown that parental supervision — in terms of knowing about the activities of teenagers when they are out with friends — is not as important in preventing delinquency among boys as might have been expected, although it was clearly an important influence on girls' delinquency. Previous studies have found a relationship between supervision and delinquency — as this study does too — but when account is taken of other aspects of family life and the lives of the teenagers supervision is not independently related to offending among boys.

We have seen from Chapter 4 that the factors relating to juvenile offending were broadly similar for boys and girls and this is consistent with other studies which have looked at both male and female delinquency (see, for example, Smith, 1979; Canter, 1982). The present study showed that having friends who are said to be delinquent, not regarding offending as particularly serious and not getting on well with their fathers, were all strongly related to offending. In addition, lax parental supervision and teenagers' poor attitudes to school were associated with girls' delinquency as was the amount of spare time spent away from the home with friends with boys' delinquency. Thus the findings do confirm that aspects of family relations *are* very important for both boys and girls. Before turning to the ways in which these, and other, findings might be translated into pointers for parental action, it seems appropriate to consider some of the problems this advice might encounter. Firstly, whether the survey findings are a useful basis for advice involves an assumption that the factors identified are in some way causally related to teenage delinquency. But one limitation of the present type of study is that in cross-sectional research (but less often in longitudinal studies) the associations uncovered are consistent . with a number of alternative interpretations and have no necessary causal implications. Moreover, the direction of causality is not inevitably indicated.

Secondly, it would be unrealistic to expect to eliminate juvenile crime completely. Decades of delinquency research have not provided any clear lines for preventive action which have been shown to be generally effective and it would be a mistake to imagine that more parental control could be the complete answer to juvenile offending. A more realistic objective might be to encourage parental awareness of the number of opportunities for offending and about the areas over which they can expect to exert some influence, particularly in the early years, and which may be important in keeping their children on the right side of the law.

Lastly, whether parents will recognise it is their teenagers who are breaking the law is uncertain. The survey shows that parents have some, albeit imprecise, idea about their children's present conduct. But, of those who have given their parents no apparent cause for concern, about half the boys and two-fifths of the girls had committed at least one offence in the 12 months prior to the survey. Again, parents' misplaced confidence is indicated by how often they are prepared to say they trust their children to keep out of trouble when they are out with their friends. Among girls who were trusted to behave more than one-third were delinquent and among boys the corresponding figure was just under one-half. Thus, it may be difficult to get parents to realise that despite their children's ostensible good behaviour, a substantial percentage are running a risk of being caught breaking the law. The tendency for parents to lay the blame for juvenile crime (much of which is trivial) on other children and their parents points to what may be a certain short-sightedness when it comes to their own teenage children. Moreover, parents may tend to believe that minor involvement in lawbreaking is for many simply part of growing up and something which does not require them to be overtly concerned.

The remainder of the present chapter is largely devoted to the study's implications for parental action. These issues are organised in five sections, three relevant to both teenage boys and girls: attitudes to crime, family relationships and choice of friends, and a further two, mainly applicable to teenage girls, concerning parental supervision and attitudes to school. The concluding section presents a brief list of measures parents might wish to consider.

Attitudes to crime

The importance of attitudes to offending indicates their pervasive influence on behaviour: one persisting across time and across different situations when away from home. Those with strong acquired inhibitions against offending will be less likely to succumb when faced with an opportunity, despite the argument that delinquent teenagers regard offending in a less serious light because they themselves have committed the offences in question (Claster, 1967; Bem, 1972). While there may be some genetic predisposition to anti-social conduct (see, for example Hutchings and Mednick, 1977), the most likely explanation of the association between attitudes and behaviour focuses on the development of children's ideas about crime, the police and the courts and in which parents must play a large part.

Moreover, parents may influence their teenagers not only by their own attitudes to crime but also by how they respond to their children's behaviour. When parents do not react swiftly and sharply to serious misbehaviour then the restraining influences which might prevent a re-occurence of the act will be less strong. A related possibility is that some parents are less observant or inquisitive than others about what their children have been up to. Loeber (1983), for example, found that the age at which parents first noticed their children had been stealing was considerably later for major than for minor delinquents. It may be important for parents, whatever their personal beliefs, to make it clear to their children that they regard breaking the law as a serious matter, rather than, say, turning a blind eye in the belief that any action will only make things worse or that the incident represents an isolated event. Making disapproval clear from an early age, rather than later in response to a discovered or suspected offence, will probably require parents to take a less optimistic view of their children's behaviour out of the home.

Family relationships

The following section is mainly concerned with two-parent families but, as Chapter 6 shows, the relevance of family relationships to delinquency is broadly similar in one-parent households and, as we have seen, teenagers living in one-parent households were no more likely to be delinquent.

The survey shows that delinquency was strongly associated with a lack of close feelings or of understanding between fathers and their teenage children. While those who were less close to their fathers spent less time in the home, this increased opportunity for offending (or decreased opportunity for contact) may be less important than the quality of the parent-child relationship itself. The apparent importance of getting on with fathers to staying out of trouble, may indicate the part played by teenagers' evaluations of their conduct in terms of how they expect their parents would react. Those who are less close to their fathers may be indifferent to their disapproval to such an extent that the possible adverse consequences of offending for the family, such as embarrassment, shame or simply "letting them down", are less salient. The present survey suggests that it is worth encouraging parents to consider the wider implications of poor relationships with their children. The effects may go beyond the immediate family and influence an important area of their childrens' lives outside the home.

This is consistent with studies of the factors which are associated with the success or failure of procedures to reduce re-offending among young offenders (see, for example, Davies, 1969; Sinclair, 1971). Davies's conclusions placed primary emphasis on the quality of the father-son relationship "easily the most important family factors in the successful avoidance of further trouble are that the father should be firm but kindly, and that there should be mutual warmth and affection between him and his son''.

While it would be unrealistic to expect all parents to get on well with their teenage children — the strains of adolescence are a well-established source of parent-child conflict (see, for example, Pasley and Gecas, 1984) — parents might consider ways of reducing the tension which is likely to arise. Parents may be attaching too great an importance to imposing their views or to bringing teenagers' behaviour into line with their expectations. Parental control over children is not necessarily compatible with good parent-child relations and it may be the latter which are more important in keeping children on the right side of the law. Negotiation of rules and expectations is likely to be a more effective strategy than confrontation (see, for example, Ely, Swift and Sutherland, 1983).

Choice of friends

The two aspects of parenting — attitudes to crime and relationships with their teenagers — which have already been discussed represent areas over which parents have some direct influence. The clearest finding, however, from the survey was that juvenile offending was most strongly related to the level of delinquency among teenagers' friends. Those who included delinquents among their friends were much more likely to be delinquent themselves. It seems probable that this also includes the effects of a number of unexamined factors, for example, teenagers' tolerance of anti-social behaviour or their favourable evaluation of those who seem less prepared to conform. Similarly, the close association between friends' and teenagers' delinquency may indicate teenagers' seeking out of opportunities for group offending. But, whatever the direction of the relationship between individual and friends' delinquency there is every reason to suppose that the more involved teenagers are with delinquent friends the more likely it is that teenagers will commit offences (Sarnecki, 1983). And this also emerged as a factor relevant to teenagers' delinquency in the present study. Indeed, the police are more likely to take action against adolescents offending in groups than against lone transgressors, so that group involvement carries an additional increase in the risk of arrest (Hindelang, 1976). There is also ample research evidence from other studies (see, for example, Gladstone, 1978), that the dynamics of group behaviour, involving teenagers out in the streets looking for something to do, facilitate offences such as vandalism. More delinquent acts are committed in groups than by lone offenders (see, for example, Erickson and Jensen, 1977). Added to this are the rewards provided for anti-social behaviour by the group in whose context offending generally takes place. For boys at least, previous studies have shown that group delinquency often provides an opportunity to acquire prestige by demonstrating 'toughness' and 'courage' (Short and Strodbeck, 1965, for example).

But while delinquency is more prevalent among teenage boys who are often out with their friends, it is unlikely that simply cutting down the time they spend in this way would have much of a direct effect. The pattern of survey findings suggests that the frequency with which teenage boys are out with their friends is, by and large, something which reflects their own interest in spending time in this way rather than their parents' views about how much time they should spend at home. Boys who tended to go out more often were, for example, more likely to have their friends into their homes, to meet several friends when they went out, and to meet their friends away from their homes. Similarly, there was no relationship — as might have been expected if teenage boys' going out was a measure of parents' control over how they spend their spare time — between going out and their account of how strict their parents were or how often they went out with their family or in the times their parents set for them to be home when they did go out. Moreover, parents rarely sanctioned their children by keeping them in.

The results of the present survey also suggest that not only is delinquency among friends important but that it also makes a difference to the chances of teenage girls' own delinquency whether their friends are likely to condone stealing.

We have already seen that, generally, parents are not particularly good judges of whether their own children have broken the law without getting caught, and there is no reason to suppose they are any more accurate when it comes to their children's friends. While parents may have some difficulty in guiding the specific choices their children make, they may be able to exert more effective influence by discouraging them from making friends with those who are prepared to violate the law. Thus, one way parents might reduce the likelihood that their children will spend time with delinquents would be to emphasise, ideally from an early age, their views about such matters as, say, anti-social behaviour. A family environment which is, for example, tolerant or even supportive of inconsiderate or aggressive behaviour is unlikely to persuade children to be critical when they encounter such conduct among their friends.

The next two factors were mainly relevant to an understanding of variations in delinquency among girls in the 14–15 age-group.

Parental supervision

Among girls the influence of parental supervision was clearly marked. At least two possible overlapping interpretations of this relationship are possible. Firstly, as Hirschi (1969) has pointed out, teenagers who are well supervised are less likely to commit delinquent acts because they feel their parents are aware of their behaviour, that is, their parents are more often "psychologically present". The same author has argued that the more children are accustomed to sharing their mental life with their parents, the more they are accustomed to seeking or getting their opinion about their activities, the more likely they are to perceive them as part of their social or psychological field, and the less likely they would be to neglect their opinion when considering an act contrary to law.

Secondly, girls whose parents are not well informed about how they are spending their time with friends are in a worse position to control what they get up to. In contrast, those who are prepared to tell their parents about what they intend to do, are unlikely to ignore a parental injunction and parental knowledge of their daughters' plans does at least provide the opportunity for changing them. This second aspect is, moreover, likely to be an important part of the relationship between supervision and delinquency. Recall that the main determinant of parental supervision was daughters' willingness to tell parents about their activities with friends — delinquents were much less forthcoming than non-delinquents. Since parents of delinquents were no less interested in knowing about how spare time was spent than other parents, the relative lack of parental awareness indicates that delinquent girls were more wary of informing their parents. This suggests parents may be able to decrease the risk of their daughters' offending by increasing their involvement in, and being less credulous about, their activities outside the home. This underlines the importance of teenagers' feeling that their lives away from the family are not separate or remote from parental influence and concern.

Attitudes to school

The relevance of school factors to delinquency has been well established and it has long been known that poor performance at school is frequently associated with, if not antecedent to, juvenile offending (see, for example, Rutter, Tizard and Whitmore, 1970; West and Farrington, 1973; Rutter, Maughan, Mortimore and Ouston, 1979). Girls who said they did not take their work at school "very seriously" were more likely to be delinquent than those with a more conventional view on this matter. While there is some evidence (see, for example, Hirschi and Hindelang, 1977) that delinquents on average tend to be less academically able than non-delinquents, their poor attitudes to school may well reflect a relative lack of interest in success at school. The survey, for example, showed that delinquents were less likely to say they thought doing well at school was important. Whether this was their feeling in advance of, or in response to, a poorer level of academic achievement (delinquents were rather less likely to say that they were doing well at school), is difficult to say. But an increase in parental support and encouragement may have a beneficial effect on the incidence of delinquency.

Perhaps the major limiting factor in this respect is that teenagers who devalue academic success are likely to have friends who share the same views. In the close environment of school, expressions of a positive attitude to school work are unlikely to receive much support from these friends. Few parents would wish to go so far as changing their daughter's school in order to create an opportunity for a re-orientation towards school work, but there are opportunities for parents to take some action. Difficulties at school may be something teenagers prefer to keep to themselves but school open days, parents' evenings and parent-teacher associations provide opportunities when parents and teachers can bring particular problems to each other's attention.

In addition, there is evidence that parents and teachers tend to have rather different views about their respective roles when it comes to children at school (see, for example, Johnson and Ransom, 1983) and parents often appear reluctant to infringe what they regard as teachers' autonomy in school. There is every reason to suppose that teachers' knowledge about the family characteristics of their pupils could generally be improved and this might have the effect of bringing early attention to those who are under-achieving or whose work is deteriorating. One example of the possibilities of greater co-operation between school and home is provided by schools who have procedures whereby parents can ring school, or vice versa, to check on their children's attendance. Similarly, greater parental interest in school matters might reduce teenagers' reluctance to mention the problems they may be having.

Integration

Thus far, the discussion has tended to treat the many possible areas of parental intervention somewhat separately. The following section attempts to draw out some of the implications of how they may be interrelated. That choice of friends, attitudes to crime and family relationships were all shown to be distinct and independent effects on the likelihood of teenage delinquency implies to some extent that improvements in any one respect should have a beneficial effect on the probability of offending. This is, however, something which remains to be empirically determined and there are reasons for supposing that changing the existing situation may often be difficult. For example, existing relationships with friends are likely to carry their own momentum which may reduce the opportunities for any radical shift. Moreover, although parents may be making a conscious effort in one direction there is no reason to expect their children to go along with them. And while getting into trouble with the police is something most parents would wish their children to avoid, teenagers themselves may be less apprehensive about this possibility before it actually happens. The degree of autonomy achieved by 14 and 15 year olds will clearly vary from family to family, teenagers with little freedom are probably least likely to be delinquent, while those with a great deal are the most likely. Having achieved a measure of independence from their families, however, makes it all the more difficult for parents to bring their influence to bear on their children.

Persuasion or organisation?

Having sketched out some of the ways parents themselves might individually contribute to reducing the delinquent behaviour of their teenagers, it seems

54

appropriate to consider whether more organised support might not be additionally effective.

Self-help groups

There is little doubt that some parents find it difficult to cope with the problems of adolescent children. There may be more scope for informal opportunities for parents, who feel that dealing with their children is getting too difficult, to share and talk over their problems with others who feel the same way. Such schemes are presently running in some areas of the country, often organised by social services departments. In addition, parents can get advice directly from social workers. Discovering that these difficulties are unlikely to be enduring or that they are not alone in feeling that they can no longer communicate with their teenagers may help to put such problems into perspective. Some researchers have gone so far as to suggest that since parents find adolescence the most difficult stage to cope with, the present emphasis on families with young children is not entirely appropriate (Pasley and Gecas, 1984).

Treatment programmes

Reviews of a number of North American studies (see, Johnson, Bird, Little and Beville, 1981, for example), have suggested that:

> Noncoercive programs to teach parents social learning theory and monitor their use of it have had favourable evaluations; they appear to be effective in reducing troublesome behaviour, at least for children aged 5 through 13. Family programs to improve parents' communication skills, enlarge opportunities for children to make contributions at home, and make expectations and discipline in that setting more consistent also appear worthwhile.

But as these authors have pointed out, such individual treatment programmes have two main difficulties which limit their usefulness as a general preventive strategy. Firstly, they are expensive and, secondly, to remain effective they must be continually repeated. Clearly, they would be inappropriate for the majority of families with delinquent children. Involvement in a programme of this nature would be most likely as a response to serious or persistent offending and as part of a sentence passed by a court.

Nevertheless, some have argued that delinquency prevention should be directed at younger children, even those of pre-school age (see, Farrington, 1983, for example). While it is possible to identify groups of children with a disproportionately high risk of delinquency (eg children of convicted parents), the associated precision is often too low to justify special treatment even when ethical objections are set aside. Moreover, there seems little likelihood of achieving the 'informed consent' of those parents whose children were selected for prevention programmes. Pre-school facilities may, however, be worthwhile as a general provision available to all children with implications for reducing the likelihood of delinquent conduct.

With older children identifying appropriate forms of intervention encounters something of a paradox. The likelihood of progress would seem to vary inversely with the apparent need for success. Johnstone (1980), for example, suggests that the influence of family variables not only varies by the type of delinquency but that it is confined to relatively non-serious offences. In the study he reports, the incidence of serious offences (robbery, larceny and burglary) was unrelated to family integration. Instead, the best indicator of such offences was a measure of "community pressure", which was based on a variety of social and economic indices.

Johnstone's conclusion was that:

Where the external environment is stable and provides safety and security, disrupted family conditions can and do generate delinquent outcomes. Where communities are crowded and deteriorated, and where the economic press of life is constant and ubiquitous, however, the net added impact of a bad family situation is minimal. Deteriorated families seem to have a stronger impact on youngsters in benign than in hostile settings.

The circumstances in which changes in family functioning could have the greatest effect may tend to be those where parents will be least ready to perceive such a need. Johnson et al. (1981) in their review of prevention strategies suggest that family treatment programmes are probably more effective with pre-delinquents than with serious offenders. Research at the Oregon Social Learning Centre (see Patterson, Chamberlain and Reid (1982), for example) working with young children and their parents has shown that it is possible to influence the occurrence of "pre-delinquency" (eg lying, truancy, fighting) by teaching parents the skills they need to cope with antisocial or disruptive behaviour.

More benefit may result from schemes which blanket particular communities as a whole or to which parents in difficulty can refer themselves. Such an approach would reach those it is most likely to help and reduce the likelihood of counter-productive effects. As was outlined earlier, however, parents can be blissfully unaware about what their own children are up to, and are likely to fail to recognise the need or the scope for changes in their own relationships with their children. But providing parents recognise sufficiently early that there is a problem, there is perhaps more than is generally realised that they can do to reduce the chances of their children (and themselves) appearing in a magistrates' court.

The wider context

So far, this discussion of family functioning in relation to delinquency and supervision has paid relatively little attention to factors outside the family, that is, the broader social and economic context of their lives. At the extreme, there is evidence, from Wilson (1980), for example, that parents whose daily existence is fraught with anxiety have less inclination or ability to deal sympathetically and patiently with their children. Similarly, the home is likely to be a less attractive or interesting place for teenage children to be.

There are some who might question whether it is even appropriate that parents should be solely responsible for their children's conduct. As crime is no longer seen as purely the responsibility of the police to deal with but instead as requiring a community-wide response (see, for example, Morris and Heal, 1981) the attempt to 'push back' responsibility for young offenders into the family might be regarded as inappropriate. For example, some of the abundant opportunities for offending which confront teenagers today could be reduced in an attempt to control juvenile crime (see, for example, Mayhew, *et al.* 1976). Owners taking greater care of their valuables and other property, more thought to using vandal-resistant equipment, increasing natural surveillance of crime-related locations could all contribute to a lessening of teenage offending. Similarly, Skolnick (1978), among others, has argued that instead of attempting to reform the family, more attention should be paid to the particular aspects of the wider economic and social system which limit parents' effectiveness in dealing with their children. Such factors as a lack of employment opportunities, poor living conditions and poverty perhaps disincline parents to encourage their children to have much respect for the existing social order.

Moreover, there is no reason to suppose that such factors affect children only through their effects on parents. For instance, there is little doubt that teenagers in their last years at school are apprehensive about their chances of finding work (about two-thirds of teenagers in the present survey were worried about their chances of getting *any* sort of job). For some this might mean greater concern to avoid trouble in order to 'keep a clean sheet', but for the greater majority there is every likelihood that their commitment to the values and conventions of the wider society and the disincentives against offending will be weakened. While many school leavers will find work before long, the substantial regional variations make it likely than in some areas the prospects are extremely bleak. Many have argued that schools could do more to de-emphasise the importance of paid employment as the ultimate goal, recognising that the present restructuring of the industrial economy means that there is unlikely to be a return to former patterns of work.

Summary: do's and don'ts

In this final section it might be helpful to summarise the implications of the survey findings for parental action. Inevitably, this involves something of an over-simplification of the subtleties of parent-child relations but could provide a starting-point for considering how such relationships might be influenced. Many parents will already be doing as much as they can along the lines indicated, so the scope for change will vary from family to family. Some parents, for example, will have encouraged their children to seek and exert their own independence, yet others will be living in circumstances in which pressures outside the home may exert an overwhelming influence on their teenagers. It seems appropriate to stress at this point that the beneficial effects of compromise and negotiated agreements will probably outweigh those, if any, of coercion and confrontation. The following suggestions are mainly intended to encourage parents, and their teenagers, to think about the implications of their behaviour for each other.

1. Parents should be aware that many teenagers are currently running a risk of getting into trouble with the police and finding themselves before the courts. Often it will be their own children who are involved in offending and parents should be prepared to accept that frequently there is a need for them to take some action.

2. Contrary to what many parents might feel, there are important areas of their childrens' lives over which they could exercise some influence to reduce offending by their children. Parents should point out to their children what could happen if they got too involved with friends who were prepared to break the law.

3. Parents should not be indifferent to unexpected or unexplained events, such as items which might have been shoplifted, behaviour which might reflect the influence of drugs or excessive drinking. They should talk over with their children the unpleasant consequences of being caught offending and of drug and alcohol abuse.

4. Parents should be prepared to respond effectively to what they may suspect are the beginnings of adolescent delinquency. Rather than ignoring it and hoping it will go away, parents should be prepared to talk over what is happening with their children.

5. Parents should make it clear that they disapprove strongly of both antisocial and criminal behaviour. Ultimately, it is the community — including parents — which has to bear the costs of offending through tax revenue expended on the police, the courts and prisons. This makes it especially important that parents should try not to adopt double standards.

6. Parents should be prepared to spend time with their teenagers. It is particularly important for fathers to be able to listen and respond sympathetically to their children's problems. Whenever possible parents should try to make the home an interesting place for their children to be. Parents whose children seem to spend little time at home might try to find out the reasons.

Perhaps their children feel that their friends are unlikely to be welcome or that their home affords them insufficient privacy.

7. Parents should try not to let relationships with their children deteriorate to the point at which no-one is talking to each other. They should be prepared to negotiate and compromise to avoid this happening.

8. If children do get into trouble with the police, parents should be prepared to be supportive and recognise that commitment to their children may influence whether they stay out of trouble in the future.

9. Parents should try to take an interest in what their children do at school and take what opportunities there are to visit the school. Parents should be prepared to talk over school and family problems with the child's teachers. Turning a blind eye to truancy or unauthorised absences is unlikely to encourage a positive attitude to school.

10. Parents should take an interest in their children's friends and in how they spend their spare time together. Children should be encouraged to be honest in this respect and to believe that parents would prefer a truthful rather than an acceptable answer.

Appendix 1
Note on survey sampling and design

(Abbreviated from a Technical Report supplied by Douglas Wood, Social and Community Planning Research.)

The final questionnaire reflected the outcome of an initial exploratory and developmental stage. This consisted of two parts: firstly, a series of individual unstructured interviews and group discussions, and secondly, piloting of a draft questionnaire in the late spring of 1983.

The main fieldwork took place between mid-June and mid-August 1983, and this involved screening a stratified random sample of 17,784 electoral register addresses to identify households where children aged 14 or 15 lived with one or both of their natural parents. At these households interviews were sought with the child and a parent. If the household contained more than one child eligible for interview a systematic method was used to select one for participation in the survey.

The decision to seek interviews with mothers rather than with fathers (except where there was no mother in the household) was based on two main considerations. Experience during the developmental phase indicated that joint parent interviews lasted rather longer than those for one parent, but contributed little additional information. Moreover, if one parent was sought for interview, parents themselves felt that the mother was the more appropriate respondent. This was particularly the case for girls.

For the purposes of the survey, parents were defined as natural parents, step-parents (including common law step-parents) and adoptive parents. It was decided that in cases where a child was living with other relatives only (e.g. grandparents or siblings) or where the child was fostered, no interview should be sought. Similarly, children living in institutions were excluded from the sample.

While the most obvious and direct method of contacting families with children in the 14–15 age group would appear to be through schools, this poses a number of practical difficulties. Previous experience has shown that there are often insurmountable obstacles to obtaining lists of addresses of school pupils, even at a local level. On a national scale, these problems become prohibitive. Instead it was decided to define the households to be screened through the electoral register. These omit about 4% of addresses of private households (Todd and Butcher, 1982) but offer the most practical sampling frame.

Based on the 1981 population census and estimates of the number of children living with siblings in the same age group, it was estimated that the proportion of households in England and Wales with children aged 14 or 15 was about 8.3%. The target sample was 1,000 double interviews, that is, family interviews from both a child and his or her parent. On the basis of the estimated prevalence of eligible households and assuming a response rate of 70%, the necessary number of addresses for screening was approximately 17,800.

Given that only about 1 in 12 households would be eligible, it was decided to screen addresses in tight clusters. Tight clustering of a sample tends to produce large design effects and reduce precision. But our concern in this case was not with the precision of the sample screened but with that of the sub-sample of eligible households indentified. And a tightly clustered screening sample for a minority population does not yield a tightly clustered subsample of that minority.

Accordingly, addresses were selected from the electoral register, not individually, but in blocks of six. The sample of addresses was selected in three stages:

i. *Selection of constituencies*
114 constituencies in England and Wales were selected with a probability proportional to their electorate after stratification by standard region, population density and percentage of the population aged under 15 at the time of the 1971 Census (1981 figures were not available at the time of sampling).

ii. *Selection of wards*
In each selected constituency, one ward (or group of wards based on combining adjacent very small wards) was selected with a probability proportionate to its electorate.

iii. *Selection of addresses*
In each selected ward or ward group, 65 elector names were selected by the random starting point and fixed interval method. The addresses shown for these names were examined and if that was not the first appearance of the address in the register it was discarded. The remaining total was then reduced to 26 by random deletion.

For each of the 26 starting addresses the next five addresses to appear in the register were also selected, giving a total of 156 addresses per ward or ward group.

Screening procedure

In a survey screening for a minority population, considerable interviewer time will be spent attempting to make contact with households the vast majority of

62

which will not be eligible for interview. As a way of reducing contacting time, the survey screening stage adopted a variant of the focused enumeration method which had previously been found to be extremely effective. Interviewers were permitted to collect information on the possible eligibility of households from their neighbours.

The procedure involved interviewers who had made contact at a household and established whether a 14 or 15 year-old lived there asking whether there were any children between 12 and 17 in the households on either side, provided these were also addresses which formed part of the sample. The wider age range was chosen to minimise the problem of mistakes over children's ages. If the respondent was unsure or said that there were such children at the address, calls were made. Otherwise the interviewer treated the adjoining address(es) as screened out.

Fieldwork results

Of the 17,784 electoral register addresses issued, 17,365 were identified as eligible for screening. Of this smaller number, 17,226 (99%) were screened, either directly or through information provided by neighbours. While it was expected that about 8.3% of households would contain a child of 14 or 15, the proportion identified by the screen was much lower at just 6.3% and did not reach the expected figure in any region of the country. The most likely explanation of this difference would seem to be a form of concealed refusal with eligible households denying having such children; a simpler way of avoiding an interview than a direct refusal.

The total number of eligible households identified through the screening process was 1,063. Double interviews were successfully carried out at 773 of these, losses in transit reduced this to an effective figure of 751.

A more detailed account of the survey fieldwork will be found in Wood (1983).

Whether the sample on which the survey findings are based is completely representative of all families in this country with children in the 14–15 age range is difficult to answer. There is no direct way of knowing the characteristics of this very much larger group particularly in relation to factors which might be important for relationships between parents and their teenagers. Families which declined to take part might well have differed in this regard from those which participated. It is possible, for example, that families whose children were more likely to be involved in delinquency were underrepresented in the study. Moreover, it is unlikely that the survey results can be simply generalised to any particular subgroup since the report reflects a wide range of family situations across the country as a whole.

Appendix 2
Alternative definitions of delinquency and supervision

The particular way delinquency and parental supervision are defined is likely to have a bearing on the outcome of any analysis. The relative importance of individual, peer group and family factors is to some extent a reflection of the particular indices chosen to represent offending and supervision. It would not be surprising if alternative measures presented a somewhat different picture of the influences on, and the effects of, these two factors.

Delinquency

Delinquency in previous analyses in the present study has consistently involved a contrast between those who had not committed any offences in the 12 months preceding the interview and those who admitted they had. This distinction, perhaps, involves the fewest arbitrary assumptions about offending. It is equally possible, however, to make other contrasts which reflect different aspects of delinquency. One, for example, might be between those who have committed "serious" offences and those who have not, or another between those who have committed relatively many and those who have committed relatively few delinquent acts. Research generally supports the idea that those who commit many offences also tend to commit the more serious offences (see, for example, West and Farrington, 1973). And for the offences most frequently admitted by the teenagers in the survey there is no completely satisfactory means of assignment to a "serious" and a "non-serious" category. For these two reasons, the alternative index of delinquency selected to re-examine the generality of the analysis reported on in Chapter 4, was based on the *number* of delinquent acts committed in the 12 months leading up to the survey. This measure of serious involvement in delinquency was constructed by identifying those teenagers who reported committing five or more offences in the relevant period. (Five offences was chosen as the threshold for this category as this was the figure which split offenders as nearly as possible into two equal groups.)

Of the 378 boys in the study 78 (21%) admitted more frequent involvement in delinquency, the corresponding figure for girls was slightly lower at 17% (64/373). Using this new definition the previous analyses of boys' and girls' delinquency were repeated to assess whether a different set of factors was associated with serious involvement in delinquency.

For boys, serious delinquency was related to friends' offending, how often they went out to see friends and not expecting to feel guilty if involved in stealing. The likelihood of involvement in serious delinquency was: about six (5.9) times greater if the teenager's friends had committed many rather than few or no delinquent acts, about five (4.7) times greater if the teenager went out three or more times a week and about three (2.7) times greater if the boy did not anticipate feeling "very guilty" if he stole. Again, there was no apparent independent effect of parental supervision on delinquency among teenage boys. This pattern of results tends to underline the importance of teenagers' friends for offending and to indicate that serious involvement in delinquency is largely independent of contemporary family factors once account has been taken of particular peer group and individual differences.

In the case of girls, serious offending was by and large associated with the same factors as distinguished delinquents from non-delinquents. The analysis showed that the likelihood of involvement in serious delinquency was: about eight (7.6) times greater if the girl's friends had committed many rather than few or no delinquent acts, about four (4.2) times greater if she did not anticipate feeling "very guilty" if she stole, about twice (2.3 times) as great if she felt her father did not understand her problems, about twice (2.3 times) as great if the girl thought it would make little difference to her friends if she stole and about twice as great if her parents did not almost always know the details of how she spends her spare time. The independent effect of parental supervision on serious delinquency among teenage girls is apparently rather less than indicated by its role in distinguishing between delinquents and non-delinquents.

Summary for delinquency

For serious delinquency among teenage boys and girls, the revised analysis indicated that the shift of focus to those more involved in offending was not accompanied by any substantial change in the range of factors associated with offending. In particular there was no evidence that parental supervision should be assigned a more central role in understanding variations in delinquent behaviour.

Supervision

Mention has already been made of some of the many different aspects of parental behaviour which researchers have utilised to construct indices of supervision. Furthermore, previous discussion has touched on the influence of children's age on how supervision is regarded. To some extent how parental supervision is measured will reflect the particular interests of the study in question. In the present case attention was directed towards teenagers many of whom were probably pushing at the limits of parental tolerance. Notions of chaperonage or confinement to the family home are clearly inappropriate for the age-group under study. Nevertheless, parental behaviour about setting times for their children to be home and expecting them home early rather than late are possible alternative or complementary aspects of supervision.

Overall, there was relatively little variation in the extent to which parents fixed a time for their children to be home either during the week or at the weekend. Those who were relatively lax about arranging a time were about equally represented among parents of delinquents and non-delinquents. Being unreliable about coming home at the arranged time, in contrast, was related to delinquency for both boys and girls. The strength of the association, however, was low (x^2 = 5.03 and 5.70 with 1 d.f., $p <$ .05, respectively) and rather weaker than that between the selected index of supervision and delinquency. It would, in addition, be difficult to justify using such an item to measure parental supervision representing as it does the behaviour of teenagers themselves.

The particular time parents set for their children to be home varied considerably between weekdays and weekends. During the week only one-third of teenagers were expected back at or after 10 pm, but at the weekend this increased to one-half. While the times fixed by parents of delinquent teenagers were generally later, only for boys was there a significant association (p < .005) with delinquency (x^2 = 8.00 and 10.36 with 1 d.f., for weekdays and weekends, respectively). Furthermore, the strength of these relationships is comparable with that between the original index of parental supervision and delinquency. The high correlation, however, between the time at which teenagers were expected home and the actual measure of parental supervision used in the analysis indicates that little would have been gained by extending the index of supervision in this way.

Summary for supervision

For 14 and 15 year-old boys and girls, a definition of parental supervision which represents their parents' awareness of how they spend their spare time is not without certain drawbacks. While it reflects a narrow aspect of parental behaviour, it probably comes closest to the way the notion of supervision is used by parents of teenagers in this age group. Alternative measures of supervision based on rules about coming home at night were shown to be either unrelated to delinquency or closely associated with the existing definition of supervision.

Appendix 3
Items used to measure delinquency

Teenagers were handed sets of 21 cards on which were printed the following items. These they sorted into two groups: one representing the acts they had ever committed and a second for those they had never carried out. For each item in the first group, the interviewer asked the teenager how many times he or she had committed the act in the previous 12 months. The numbers of teenagers admitting having committed each act during this period are shown separately for boys and girls.

		Boys (N = 378)	Girls (N = 373)
1.	Smashed bottles in the street	81	31
2.	Travelled on a bus or train without a ticket or deliberately paid the wrong fare	74	67
3.	Pinched something worth less than £1 from a shop	47	22
4.	Carried a weapon (e.g. a knife) intending to use it against someone if necessary	47	17
5.	Deliberately damaged school property	45	43
6.	Broken windows in an empty house	43	12
7.	Bought something you knew had been pinched	40	12
8.	Pinched something from family or relatives	30	33
9.	Written or sprayed paint on buildings	26	45
10.	Dialled 999 as a joke	19	19
11.	Damaged seats on buses and trains	10	23
12.	Pinched something worth between £1 and £5 from a shop	9	5
13.	Pinched something worth more than £5 from a shop	9	5
14.	Taken a bicycle with no intention of putting it back	8	3

15.	Got money from someone outside the family by threats	7	5
16.	Taken money from someone outside the family by force	4	5
17.	Pinched something from a parked car	4	3
18.	Deliberately damaged a parked car	3	3
19.	Tried to set fire to a building	1	1
20.	Snatched someone's wallet or handbag	1	1
21.	Got into someone's home while they were out and pinched something	0	1

Appendix 4
Part A: Survey factors related to delinquency

KEY
***** = p < .001
**** = p < .005
*** = p < .01
** = p < .025
* = p < .05

Boys

Family differences
Delinquent boys:

— more often had parents who worried about what they got up to in their spare time (*****)
— more often felt they were not very close to their father (****)
— more often had fathers who were not very close to their sons (****)
— less often were well supervised (****)
— more often were allowed to come home late (****)
— less often went out with their parents as a family group (****)
— more often had tellings off from their parents (***)
— more often had rows with their parents about who they met (***) and what they did with their friends (**)
— less often felt their fathers understood their problems (**)
— more often had parents who said their sons were unreliable about coming home at sensible times (**)
— more often had parental discussions about sex (**) and drug-taking (*****)
— less often had their father living in the household (*)
— more often had mothers who felt that they wanted to spend extra time with their sons (*)
— more often had grown less close to their fathers over the previous 12 months (*)
— more often were known by their parents to have offended (*)

School differences
Delinquent boys:

— less often took their work at school seriously (*****)
— less often felt they were doing well at school (*****)
— more often were careless with their homework (*****)
— more often had to be pushed to do their homework (*****)

69

— more often played truant from school (*****)
— more often were interested in leaving school at 16 (*****)
— less often felt that doing well at school was important (****)
— more often had parent-teacher discussions about their behavioural problems at school (***)
— more often disliked school (**)
— less often talked with their parents about school (*)

Friends/going out differences
Delinquent boys:

— more often had friends who had committed criminal offences (*****)
— more often had friends to whom it would make no difference if they stole (*****)
— more often had a girlfriend (*****)
— more often went out with their friends (*****)
— more often met their friends in groups (*****)
— more often met their friends away from their homes (***)
— more often spent their spare time away from their home (**)
— more often had had friends whom their parents thought "undesirable" (**)
— more often met their friends in mixed groups (**)
— more often had friends who regarded doing well at school as unimportant (**)

Belief differences
Delinquent boys:

— less often expected to feel guilty if they stole (*****)
— less often expected being convicted of stealing would make a difference either to their friends (*****) or at school (***)
— less often thought stealing was a serious offence (****)
— less often expected to be caught if they did steal (**)

Police contact differences
Delinquent boys:

— more often had been stopped on the street and asked questions by the police (*****)
— less often thought that the police in their area treated teenagers fairly (**)
— more often had reported a crime to the police (**)
— more often had asked for help from the police (*)

Girls

Family differences
Delinquent girls:

— less often felt their mothers or their fathers understood their problems or difficulties (*****)

70

— less often were willing to tell their parents about how they spent their spare time (*****)
— less often said they were closest to their fathers (*****)
— less often were well supervised (*****)
— less often went out with the family as a group (*****)
— more often had mothers who worried about what they got up to in their spare time (****)
— less often shared an interest or hobby with their fathers (****)
— more often attempted to play one parent off against the other (****)
— less often were trusted by their parents to behave themselves when out with their friends (****)
— more often said it was their mothers who were "easiest" on them (****)
— more often had parents who felt that they wanted to spend extra time with their daughters (****)
— more often had rows with their parents about who they spent their time with (****), the things they did with their friends (***) and the time they were expected home in the evenings (*****)
— more often had grown less close to their mothers over the previous 12 months (***)
— less often talked over with their parents what they might do when they left school (***)
— more often chatted mostly to their mothers (***)
— less often felt "very close" either to their mothers (**) or to their fathers (***)
— more often had parents who thought they were more lenient than average (**)
— more often complained that they were being treated unfairly (*)
— more often had parents who had a poor opinion of their neighbourhood (*)
— more often had, and previously had, friends their parents thought "undesirable" (*)
— more often had rows with their parents over clothes, jewellery, make-up, hairstyle (*)

School differences
Delinquent girls:

— less often took their work at school or their homework seriously (*****)
— more often played truant from school (*****)
— less often felt that doing well at school was important (*****)
— more often had friends who thought that doing well at school was not important (*****)
— more often disliked school (****)
— less often went straight home after school (*)

71

Friends/going out differences
Delinquent girls:

— more often spent their spare time away from their home (*****)
— more often went out with their friends (*****)
— more often met their friends in mixed groups (*****)
— more often had a boyfriend (*****)
— more often were thought by their parents to be likely to get into trouble with the police in the next few years (*****)
— more often had friends who were themselves delinquent (*****)
— more often had friends to whom it would make no difference if they stole (*****)
— more often were unreliable about coming home in the evening (**)
— more often had friends who thought that looking grown-up (*) and keeping up with the charts were important (**)

Belief differences
Delinquent girls:

— less often thought that stealing was serious (*****)
— less often expected that they would feel guilty if they stole (*****)
— less often expected to be upset by the sentence they would get if they were convicted of a stealing offence (*****)
— less often expected to be caught if they stole (***)
— more often expected to be taken to court if they were caught stealing (*)

Police contact differences
Delinquent girls:

— more often had been stopped on the street and questioned by the police (*****)
— less often thought the police in their area treated young people fairly (*****)
— more often had reported a crime (****)
— more often had reported some other problem (****)
— more often had asked for help (**)
— more often had asked for directions from the police (*)

Appendix 4
Part B: Survey factors unrelated to delinquency

Although the analysis of the survey results does point to important differences between delinquent and non-delinquent teenagers, it seems worthwhile to bear in mind the degree to which the characteristics of these two groups overlapped. In interpreting the survey findings there is a danger of overlooking the degree of similarity in the individual and family characteristics of delinquents and non-delinquents. It may be useful to describe briefly some of these areas which appeared unrelated to delinquency to counter the notion that the characteristics of delinquent teenagers were uniformly different.

Non-correlates of delinquency among boys

Whether boys were 14 or 15 made no difference to their chances of being delinquent. Nor was this associated with the size of the boy's family, whether his mother worked or with the family's socio-economic group.

Moreover, parents of delinquent boys were no less likely to know their sons' friends by name, to trust them to behave when out with their friends, to feel they should know about the details of how he spends his spare time, to have sons who were willing to tell them about their spare time activities, to fix a time for their sons to be home in the evenings. Delinquent boys and their friends were equally interested in sport, in pop music, in looking grown-up and in wearing fashionable clothes.

It appeared to make little difference to delinquency whether sons shared an interest or hobby with either of their parents, whether sons felt their mothers understood their problems, whether mothers felt particularly close to their sons, whether sons were prepared to bring their problems to their parents, whether sons were talkative or reticent, whether sons had rows with their parents over their appearance, over the time they came home at night, over who they spent their spare time with, over how they spent their pocket money. Similarly, there was no association between delinquency and whether parents were stricter than average, whether their sons were thought to be particularly mature compared with their friends or were thought to want their own way more than average, whether sons tried to play one parent off against the other, whether sons thought that they were being treated unfairly compared with their friends, whether parents thought their sons were likely to get into trouble with the police in the future. Delinquent boys were no less likely to do regular chores around the home, nor were they any less diligent in this respect.

In relation to school, the survey revealed no association between delinquency and size or type of school, whether single-sex or co-ed, parents' views about the teachers or the discipline at their sons' school, the amount of homework their sons did, whether or not boys came straight home after school.

Non-correlates of delinquency among girls

Girls of 15 were no more likely to be delinquent than those of 14, nor was there an association with whether her father lived in the household, or with the size of her family, or with whether her mother worked, or with the family's socio-economic group.

In relation to the child's friends, it seemed to matter little whether she met her friends in a group, the sorts of values she and her friends seemed to have when it came to their appearance or the importance of having money, whether parents knew her friends by name, whether they fixed a time for her to be home in the evenings, whether she was expected home by 10 pm or not or whether she met her friends at their homes or elsewhere, whether she was a member of a club, group or society.

Similarly, there was no indication from the survey that delinquency was related to how close her mother felt to her, whether she shared an interest or hobby with her mother, whether she felt closer to one or other of her parents or equally close to both, whether or not she did chores around the house nor how well she did them, whether her parents felt they should know the details of how she spent her time with her friends, the frequency of tellings off she got, parents' feelings that she wanted her own way more than average, whether she was prepared to take her problems to her mother, whether she was a talkative or an unresponsive child.

In the area of school factors, delinquency did not appear to be associated with her account of how well she was doing at school, the type or size of school she attended or whether it was a single-sex or co-ed school, the way her parents felt about the staff or the discipline at her school or how often they had visited it, the amount of time she spent on her homework or how often her parents had to push her to do her homework, or her interest in leaving school at 16.

74

Appendix 5
A note on logistic regression

Briefly, the aim of the analysis of the survey data was to examine whether variations between teenagers in parental supervision were related to delinquency after allowing for the effects of other possible influences on offending. The influence of these factors is indicated by the "goodness of fit" or G-square statistic which has an approximate chi-square distribution. The comparative size of the reduction in G-square provides an estimate of the relative importance of each factor or combination of factors in understanding differences in delinquency. Bishop *et al.* (1975) carries a description of the log linear modelling procedure.

The statistical technique selected as the most appropriate was logistic regression (or linear-logistic analysis), which is based on the generalised linear model — GLIM (see, for example, Baker and Nelder, 1978). Logistic regression is designed for data where the response variable takes a binary form (as in the present survey in which delinquency is categorised into two levels). This form of analysis fits a model to the data which maximises the amount of variation explained in delinquency by including in the model those factors which produce the largest reductions in unexplained variation (that is, in scaled deviance or G-square). The general method was to examine the improvement in the fit of the model taking one factor at a time, but in the initial stages of the model-building process to omit consideration of parental supervision. Thus, the first factor to be fitted to the model was that which was associated with the largest reduction in scaled deviance. The second factor to be fitted was that which produced the largest reduction in scaled deviance when added to a model containing the first factor. This process, including an assessment of interaction effects, was continued in a stepwise manner until no further variables significantly improved the fit of the model. At this point, it was possible to evaluate the independent effect of including in the model the factor representing parental supervision.

Clearly, the analysis does not allow any conclusions to be drawn about how differences in parental supervision may influence delinquency indirectly through their effects on other delinquency-related aspects of teenagers' lives. The factors which are present in the logistic regression model before the direct influence of parental supervision is examined can be considered as the "background" against which the effects of supervision are looked at. Thus, the focus of the analysis is to take the personal, social and family characteristics of teenagers as given and then to assess the direct and independent effects of differences in parental supervision.

The data analysis was made more complex by the existence of missing data. An initial logistic regression was carried out on a subset which excluded cases with any data missing from the analysis variables. Then, having fitted a model, the importance of its component factors was assessed on a larger data set which excluded only those cases with missing data on the smaller number of variables actually included in the model. Whether the original model was still relevant to the larger sample was examined in two ways. By both the significance of the fit of the model and by the 'backwards elimination' of each of the components. Components which did not significantly decrease the fit of the model when eliminated were deleted.

Appendix 6
Factors associated with parental supervision

Boys

Family differences:
Poor/low supervision was associated with:

— sons being unwilling to tell their parents about how they spend their time with their friends (*****)
— parents who worry about what their sons are up to when they are out with their friends (*****)
— parents who don't feel they can trust their sons to behave themselves when they are out with their friends (*****)
— sons who are less likely to chat with both their parents (*****)
— parents who have a poor view of their neighbourhood (*****)
— parents who more often have rows with their sons over their appearance (****)
— sons who frequently get a telling off from their parents (****)
— sons who more often complain that they are treated unfairly in comparison with their friends (***)
— parents who are less likely to believe that their sons will keep out of trouble with the police in the next few years (***)
— parents who feel it would be difficult to keep their sons in if they had to (**)
— Low supervision is also associated with tenure (****) and social class (****)

Friends/going out differences:
Poor/low supervision was associated with:

— sons who often go out to see their friends (*****)
— sons who are unreliable about coming home (*****)
— sons who meet their friends in groups of four or more (*****)
— sons who have had 'undesirable' friends in the past (****)
— sons who are delinquent (****)

— sons who have rows with their parents over the way they spend their time with their friends (****)
— sons who are interested in girlfriends (***)
— sons who tend to meet their friends away from their homes (**)
— sons who were poorly supervised were more likely to have been stopped on the street and questioned by the police (*****)

School differences:
Poor/low supervision was associated with:

— parents who do not expect their sons to continue in full-time education once they reach 16 (*****)
— sons who are less likely to get homework from school (****)
— sons who are careless over their homework (****)
— sons who play truant from school (****)
— sons who don't take their work at school seriously (****)
— sons who attach less importance to doing well at school (****)
— parents who are uncertain whether their sons will sit any exams at school (***)
— parents who feel that the discipline at their sons' schools is not strict enough (**)
— parents who have a relatively poor opinion of the teachers at their sons' schools (**)
— sons who spend less time on their homework (**)

Belief differences:
Poor/low supervision was associated with:
— sons who were less likely to feel that stealing was very serious (**)
— sons who thought that being convicted of theft would not make much difference to how they were treated at school (**) or to how their friends felt about them (**)

Girls

Family differences:
Poor/low supervision was associated with:
— daughters being unwilling to tell their parents about how they spend their time with their friends (*****)
— daughters being less willing to discuss their problems or difficulties with their parents (*****)
— daughters being less likely to share a hobby or interest with their mothers (*****)
— parents who were less likely to expect that their daughters would stay out of trouble with the police over the next few years (*****)
— parents who were more likely to think it unfair for parents to be made responsible for fines imposed on their daughters (*****)

78

— parents who had a relatively poor view of the neighbourhood in which they lived (*****)
— daughters who were less likely to go out with their families (*****)
— also highly significantly associated with differences in supervision are tenure (*****) and age at which mothers left school (*****) and the age at which fathers left school (**)
— mothers being less likely to feel "very close" to their daughters (****)
— daughters being less likely to share an interest or hobby with their father (****)
— daughters who are more likely to be said to want their own way more than average (****)
— daughters who are more likely to get a telling off from their parents (****)
— daughters whose parents expect it would be relatively difficult to keep them in if they had to (****)
— daughters who are less likely to have talked with their parents about the sort of work they might do when they leave school (****)
— measures of mothers' and fathers' social class (I + II vs III + IV + V) are also significantly associated with variations in supervision (p < . 005). Social classes I and II being more likely to say they exert high supervision.
— daughters who were less likely to chat with their mothers (***)
— daughters who were more likely to try to play one parent off against the other (***)
— daughters who were more likely to complain to their parents that they were being treated unfairly compared with their friends (***)
— fathers who were less likely to be "very close" to their daughters (**)
— daughters who were less likely to have discussed how they were getting on at school with their parents (**)
— daughters who are less likely to do regular chores to help around the house (**)

Friends/going out differences:
Poor/low supervision was associated with:

— daughters who often go out to see their friends (*****)
— daughters who often have friends to their home (*****)
— parents who worry what their daughters are up to with their friends (*****)
— parents who are less likely to trust their daughters to behave themselves when out with their friends (*****)
— daughters who are less reliable about coming home at what their parents call a sensible time (*****)
— daughters who have rows with their parents about going out (*****)
— daughters who have rows with their parents about the time they should be home (*****)

79

— daughters who are more likely to be interested in boyfriends (*****)
— daughters who are likely to be delinquent (*****)
— parents who are less likely to know their daughters' friends by name (****)
— daughters whose friends were more likely to be delinquent (**)
— daughters who have had friends in the past whom their parents thought undesirable (**)

School differences:
Poor/low supervision was associated with:

— daughters who more often dislike school (*****)
— daughters who are more likely to play truant from school (*****)
— parents who are less likely to expect their daughters to continue in full-time education (*****)
— daughters who are less likely to feel that doing well at school is important (*****)
— daughters who are more likely to be careless about their homework (****)
— daughters who are less likely to take their work at school seriously (****)
— daughters whose friends are less likely to feel that doing well at school is important (****)
— daughters who are more likely to attend a comprehensive school (***)
— daughters who are less likely to spend 5 or more hours a week on their homework (**)

Police factors:
Poor/low supervision was associated with:

— daughters who are more likely to have been stopped on the street and asked questions by the police (*****)
— daughters who are more likely to think that the police treat young people in their locality unfairly (****)

80

References

Aitken, P.P. (1978). *Ten-to-Fourteen-Year-Olds and Alcohol: a developmental study in the Central Region of Scotland.* Volume III. Edinburgh: HMSO.

Bahr, S.J. (1979). 'Family determinants and the effects of deviance'. In Burr, W.R., Hill, R., Nye, F.I. and Reiss, I.L. (Eds.), *Contemporary Theories about the Family: research-based theories, Vol.1.* New York: Free Press; London: Collier-Macmillan.

Baker, R.J. and Nelder, J.A. (1978). *The GLIM System: Release 3. Generalised linear interactive modelling manual.* Oxford: NAG.

Banks, C., Maloney, E. and Willcock, H.D. (1975). 'Public attitudes to crime and the penal system'. *British Journal of Criminology,* 15, pp.228-240.

Belson, W.A. (1975). *Juvenile Theft: the causal factors.* London: Harper and Row.

Bem, D.J. (1972). 'Constructing cross-situational consistencies in behaviour: some thoughts on Alker's critique of Mischel'. *Journal of Personality,* 42, pp. 155-162.

Bishop, Y.M.M., Fienberg, S.E. and Holland, F.W. *(1975). Discrete Multivariate Analysis.* Massachusetts Institute of Technology Press.

Black, D. (1982). 'Misuse of solvents'. *Health Trends,* 14.

Bronfenbrenner, U. (1971). *Two Worlds of Childhood.* London: George Allen and Unwin.

Bynner, J.M. (1969). *The Young Smoker.* Government Social Survey. London: HMSO.

Campbell, A (1981). *Girl Delinquents.* Oxford: Basil Blackwell.

Canter, R.J. (1982). 'Family correlates of male and female delinquency'. *Criminology,* 20, pp.149-167.

Claster, D.S. (1967). 'Comparisons of risk perception between delinquents and non-delinquents'. *Journal at Criminal Law, Criminology and Police Science,* 58, pp.80-86.

Cohen, L.E. and Felson, M. (1979). 'Social change and crime rate trends: a routine activity approach'. *American Sociological Review,* 44, pp.588-608.

Davies, M. (1969). *Probationers in their Social Environment.* Home Office Research Study No. 2. London: HMSO.

Dorn, N. and Thompson, A. (1975). *A comparison of 1973 and 1974 Levels of Mid-Teenage Experimentation With Illegal Drugs In Some Schools In England.* London: Institute for the Study of Drug Dependence.

Ely, P., Swift, A. and Sutherland, A. (1983). "The 'Medway Close Support Unit: an alternative to custody for juveniles'. *Research Bulletin 16,* pp.42-44. London: Home Office.

Erickson, M.L. and Jensen, G.F. (1977). 'Delinquency is still group behaviour!' *Journal of Criminal Law and Criminology,* 68, pp.262-273.

Farrington, D.P. (1983). *Further Analyses of a Longitudinal Survey of Crime and Delinquency. Final report to the National Institute of Justice. Washington D.C. See also: 'Delinquency prevention in the 1980's.' Journal of Adolescence in press.'*

Felson, M. and Gottfredson, M. (1984). 'Social indicators of adolescent activities near peers and parents: evidence of a secular trend'. *Journal of Marriage and the Family. August,* pp.704-714.

Fogelman, K. (1978). 'Drinking among sixteen-year-olds'. *Concern,* 29, pp.19-25. London: National Children's Bureau.

Gath, D. Gattoni, F. and Rockett, D. (1977). *Child Guidance and Delinquency in a London Borough.* Oxford: Oxford University Press.

Gladstone, F. (1978). 'Vandalism among adolescent schoolboys'. In Clarke, R.V.G. (Ed.), *Tackling Vandalism.* Home Office Research Study No. 47. London: HMSO.

Glueck, S. and Glueck, E. (1950). *Unravelling Juvenile Delinquency.* Cambridge, Mass: Harvard University Press.

Henry, S. (1978). *The Hidden Economy: the context and control of borderline crime.* London: Martin Robertson.

Hindelang, M.J. (1971). 'Age, sex and versatility of delinquent involvements'. *Social Problems,* 18, pp.522-535.

Hindelang, M.J. (1976). 'With a little help from their friends: group participation in reported delinquent behaviour'. *British Journal of Criminology,* 16, pp.109-125.

Hindelang, M.J., Hirschi, T. and Weiss, J.G. (1981). *Measuring Delinquency.* London: Sage.

Hirschi, T. (1969). *Causes of Delinquency.* Berkeley: University of California Press.

Hirschi, T. and Hindelang, M.J. (1977). 'Intelligence and delinquency: a revisionist review'. *American Sociological Review,* 42, pp.571-587.

Hough, M. and Mayhew, P. (1983). *The British Crime Survey: first report.* Home Office Research Study No. 76. London: HMSO.

Hutchings, B. and Mednick, S.A. (1977). 'Criminality in adoptees and their adoptive and biological parents'. In Christiansen, K.O. and Mednick, S.A.

(S.A. (Eds.), *Biological Bases of Criminal Behaviour*. New York: Gardner Press.

Jackson, B. (1982). 'Single-parent families'. In Rapoport, R.N., Fogarty, M.P. and Rapoport, R. (Eds.), *Families In Britain*. London: Routledge and Kegan Paul.

Johnson, D. and Ransom, E. (1983). *Family and school*. London: Croom Helm.

Johnson, G., Bird, T. Little, J.W. and Beville, S.L (1981). *Delinquency preventation: theories and strategies*. Prepared for: Office of Juvenile Justice and Delinquency Prevention, U.S. Department of Justice.

Johnstone, R.E. (1980). 'Social class and delinquent behaviour'. *Criminology*, 18, pp.86-93.

Loeber, R. (1983). Personal communication.

Lewis, C., Newson, E. and Newson, J. (1982). 'Father participation through childhood and its relationship with career aspirations and delinquency'. In Beail, N. and McGuire, J. (Eds.), *Fathers. psychological perspectives*. London: Junction Books.

Mayhew, P., Clarke, R.V.G., Sturman, A. and Hough, J.M. (1976). *Crime as Opportunity*. Home Office Research Study No. 34. London: HMSO.

Medrich, E.A., Roizen, A.L. Rubin, B.C. and Buckley, C.B. (1982). *The Serious Business of Growing Up: a study of children's lives outside school*. London: University of California Press.

Morris, P. and Heal, K. (1981). *Crime Control and the Police: a review of research*. Home Office Research Study No. 67. London: HMSO.

Murdock, G. (1979). *Adolescent Culture and the Mass Media*. Research Report No. HR 1582. London: Social Science Research Council.

Newson, J. and Newson, E. (1968). *Four Years Old in an Urban Community*. London: George Allen and Unwin.

Nissel, M. (1982). 'Families and Social Change Since the Second World War'. In Rapoport, R.N., Fogarty, M.P. and Rapoport, R. (Eds.), *Families In Britain*. London: Routledge and Kegan Paul.

Office of Population Census and Surveys. (1983). *Smoking Among Adolescent School Children*. London: HMSO.

Patterson, G.R., Chamberlain, P. and Reid, J.B. (1982). 'A comparative evaluation of a parent-training program'. *Behaviour Therapy*, 13,pp.638-650.

Pasley, K. and Gecas, V. (1984). *Personnel and Guidance Journal*, 62, p. 400.

Pearson, G. (1983). *Hooligan: a history of respectable fears*. London: The Macmillan Press.

Power, M.J., Alderson, M.R., Phillipson, C.M., Schoenberg, E. and Morris, J.N. (1967). 'Delinquent schools?' *New Society,* 10, pp. 542-543.

Rankin, J.H. (1983). 'The family context of delinquency'. *Social Problems,* 30, pp. 466-479.

Research Bureau Limited. (1979). *Evaluation of an Anti-Vandalism Advertising Campaign.* Prepared for the Central Office of Information. Job No. 11500.

Reynolds, D. and Jones, D. (1978). 'Education and the prevention of juvenile delinquency: In Tutt, N. (Ed.), *Alternative Stategies For Coping With Crime.* Oxford: Blackwell.

Rimmer, L. (1981). *Families in Focus.* Occasional Paper No.6. London: Study Commission on the Family.

Rimmer, L. and Popay, J. (1982). *Employment Trends and the Family.* Occasional Paper No.10. London: Study Commission on the Family.

Rutter, M. and Giller, H. (1983). *Juvenile Delinquency: trends and perspectives.* London: Penguin.

Rutter, M., Maughan, B., Mortimore, P. and Ouston, J. (1979). *Fifteen Thousand Hours.* Shepton Mallet: Open Books.

Rutter, M., Tizard, J. and Whitmore, K. (Eds). (1970). *Education, Health and Behaviour.* London: Longmans.

Sarnecki, J. (1983). *Leisure and Criminality.* Report for the National Council for Crime Prevention, Sweden.

Shapland, J.M. (1978). 'Self-reported delinquency in boys aged 11 to 14'. *British Journal of Criminology,* 18, pp.255-266;

Short, J.F. Jr. and Strodbeck, F.L. (1965). *Group Processes and Gang Delinquency.* Chicago: University of Chicago Press.

Sinclair, I. (1971). *Hostels for Probationers.* Home Office Research Study No.6. London: HMSO.

Skolnick, A. (1978). *The Intimate Environment.* Boston: Little, Brown and Co.

Smart, C. and Smart, B. (Eds.) (1978). *Women Sexuality and Social Control.* London: Routledge and Kegan Paul.

Smelser, N. (1982). 'The Victorian family'. In Rapoport, R.N., Fogarty, M.P. and Rapoport, R. (Eds.), *Families In Britain.* London: Routledge and Kegan Paul.

Smith, D.A. (1979). 'Sex and deviance: an assessment of major sociological variables'. *The Sociological Quarterly,* 20, pp.183-195.

Study Commission on the Family. (1982). *Values and the Changing Family: a final report from the working party on values.* London.

Todd, J. and Butcher, B. (1982). *Electoral Registration in 1981.* Office of Population Censuses and Surveys. London: HMSO.

Thornton, W.E. and James, J. (1979). 'Masculinity and delinquency revisited'. *British Journal of Criminology,* 19, pp.225-241.

Wadsworth, M. (1979). *Roots of Delinquency.* London: Martin Robertson.

Walker, M.A. (1983). 'Self-report crime studies and the British Crime Survey'. *The Howard Journal of Penology and Crime Prevention,* 22, pp.168-176.

West, D.J. (1969). *Present Conduct and Future Delinquency.* London: Heinemann Educational Books.

West, D.J. (1982). *Delinquency: its roots, careers and prospects.* London: Heinemann.

West, D.J. and Farrington, D.P. (1973). *Who Becomes Delinquent?* London: Heinemann Educational.

West, D.J. and Farrington, D.P. (1977). *The Delinquent Way of Life.* London: Heinemann Educational.

Willmott, P. and Willmott, P. (1982). 'Children and family diversity'. In Rapoport, R.N., Fogarty, M.P. and Rapoport, R.(Eds.), *Families In Britain.* London: Routledge and Kegan Paul.

Wilson, H. (1980). 'Parental supervision: a neglected aspect of delinquency'. *British Journal of Criminology,* 20, pp. 203-235.

Wilson, H. (1982). 'Parental responsibility and delinquency: reflections on a White Paper proposal'. *The Howard Journal of Penology and Crime Prevention.* 21, pp. 23-34.

Wilson, H. and Herbert, G.W. (1978). *Parents and Children in the Inner City.* London: Routledge and Kegan Paul.

Wood, D. (1984). *Delinquency and Parental Supervision of Teenagers: technical note.* London: Social and Community Planning Research.

Publications

*Out of print.

6. *Hostels for probationers. A study of the aims, working and variations in effectiveness of male probation hostels with special reference to the influence of the environment on delinquency. Ian Sinclair. 1971. ix + 200pp. (11 340106 X).

7. *Prediction methods in criminology—including a prediction study of young men on probation. Frances H. Simon. 1971. xi + 234pp. (11 340107 8).

8. *Study of the juvenile liaison scheme in West Ham 1961-65. Marilyn Taylor. 1971. vi + 46pp. (11 340108 6).

9. *Exploration in after-care. I—After-care units in London, Liverpool and Manchester. Martin Silberman (Royal London Prisoners' Aid Society) and Brenda Chapman. II—After-care hostels receiving a Home Office grant. Ian Sinclair and David Snow (HORU). III—St. Martin of Tours House. Aryeh Leissner (National Bureau for Co-operation in Child Care). 1971. xi + 140pp. (11 340109 4).

10. A survey of adoption in Great Britain. Eleanor Grey in collaboration with Ronald M. Blunden. 1971. ix + 168pp. (11 340110 8).

11. *Thirteen-year-old approved school boys in 1962. Elizabeth Field, W.H. Hammond and J. Tizard. 1971. ix + 46pp. (11 340111 6).

12. Absconding from approved schools. R.V.G. Clarke and D.N. Martin. 1971. vi + 146pp. (11 340112 4).

13. An experiment in personality assessment of young men remanded in custody. H. Sylvia Anthony. 1972. viii + 79pp. (11 340113 2).

14. *Girl offenders aged 17-20 years. I—Statistics relating to girl offenders aged 17-20 years from 1960 to 1970. II—Re-offending by girls released from borstal or detention centre training. III —The problems of girls released from borstal training during their period on after-care. Jean Davies and Nancy Goodman. 1972. v + 77p. (11 340114 0).

15. *The controlled trial in institutional research—paradigm or pitfall for penal evaluators? R.V.G. Clarke and D.B. Cornish. 1972. v + 33pp. (11 340115 9).

16. *A survey of fine enforcement. Paul Softley. 1973. v + 65pp. (11 340116 7).

17. *An index of social environment—designed for use in social work research. Martin Davies. 1973. vi + 63pp. (11 340117 5).

18. *Social enquiry reports and the probation service. Martin Davies and Andrea Knopf. 1973. v + 49pp. (11 340118 3).

19. *Depression, psychopathic personality and attempted suicide in a borstal sample. H. Sylvia Anthony. 1973. viii + 44pp. (0 11 340119 1).

20. *The use of bail and custody by London magistrates' courts before and after the Criminal Justice Act 1967. Frances Simon and Mollie Weatheritt. 1974. vi + 78pp. (0 11 340120 5).

21. *Social work in the environment. A study of one aspect of probation practice. Martin Davies, with Margaret Rayfield, Alaster Calder and Tony Fowles. 1974. ix + 151pp. (0 11 340121 3).

22. Social work in prison. An experiment in the use of extended contact with offenders. Margaret Shaw. 1974. viii + 154pp. (0 11 340122 1).

23. Delinquency amongst opiate users. Joy Mott and Marylin Taylor. 1974. vi + 31pp. (0 11 340663 0).

24. IMPACT. Intensive matched probation and after-care treatment. Vol. I—The design of the probation experiement and an interim evaluation. M.S. Folkard, A.J. Fowles, B.C. McWilliams, W. McWilliams, D.D. Smith, D.E. Smith and G.R. Walmsley. 1974. v + 54pp. (0 11 340664 9).

25. The approved school experience. An account of boys' experiences of training under differing regimes of approved schools, with an attempt to evaluate the effectiveness of that training. Anne B. Dunlop. 1974. vii + 124pp. (0 11 340665 7).

26. *Absconding from open prisons. Charlotte Banks, Patricia Mayhew and R.J. Sapsford. 1975 viii + 89pp. (0 11 340666 5).

27. Driving while disqualified. Sue Kriefman. 1975. vi + 136pp. (0 11 340667 3).

*Out of print.

28. Some male offenders' problems. I—Homeless offenders in Liverpool. W. McWilliams. II— Casework with short-term prisoners. Julie Holborn. 1975. x + 147pp. (0 11 340668 1).

29. *Community service orders. K. Pease, P.Durkin, I. Earnshaw, D. Payne and J. Thorpe. 1975. viii + 80pp. (0 11 340669 X).

30. Field Wing Bail Hostel: the first nine months. Frances Simon and Sheena Wilson. 1975. viii + 55pp. (0 11 340670 3).

31. Homicide in England and Wales 1967-1971. Evelyn Gibson. 1975. iv + 59pp. (0 11 340753 X).

32. Residential treatment and its effects on deliquency. D.B. Cornish and R.V.G. Clarke. 1975. vi + 74pp. (0 11 340672 X).

33. Further studies of female offenders. Part A: Borstal girls eight years after release. Nancy Goodman, Elizabeth Maloney and Jean Davies. Part B: The sentencing of women at the London Higher Courts. Nancy Goodman, Paul Durkins and Janet Halton. Part C: Girls appearing before a juvenile court. Jean Davies. 1976. vi + 114pp. (0 11 340673 8).

34. *Crime as opportunity. P. Mayhew, R.V.G. Clarke, A. Sturman and J.M. Hough. 1976. vii + 36pp. (0 11 340674 6).

35. The effectiveness of sentencing: a review of the literature. S.R. Brody. 1976. v + 89pp. (0 ⁻11 340675 4).

36. IMPACT. Intensive matched probation and after-care treatment. Vol II—The results of the experiment. M.S. Folkard, D.E. Smith and D.D. 1976 xi + 400pp. (0 11 340676 2).

37. Police cautioning in England and Wales. J.A. Ditchfield. 1976. v + 31pp. (0 11 340677 0).

38. Parole in England and Wales. C.P. Nuttall, with E.E. Barnard, A.J. Fowles, A. Frost, W. H. Hammond, P. Mayhew, K. Pease, R. Tarling and M.J. Weatheritt, 1977. vi + 90pp. (0 11 340678 9).

39. Community service assessed in 1976. Pease, S. Billingham and I. Earnshaw. 1977. vi + 29pp. (0 11 340679 7).

40. Screen violence and film censorship: a review of research. Stephen Brody. 1977. vii + 179pp. (0 11 340680 0).

41. Absconding from borstals. Gloria K. Laycock. 1977. v + 82pp. (0 11 340681 9).

42. Gambling: a review of the literature and its implications for policy and research. D.B. Cornish. 1978. xii + 284pp. (0 11 340682 7).

43. Compensation orders in magistrates' courts. Paul Softley. 1978. v + 41pp. (0 11 340683 5).

44. Research in criminal justice. John Croft. 1978. iv + 16pp. (0 11 340684 3).

45. Prison welfare: an account of ana experiment at Liverpool. A.J. Fowles. 1978. v + 34pp. (0 11 340685 1).

46. Fines in magistrates' courts. Paul Softley. 1978. v + 42pp. (0 11 340686 X).

47. Tackling vandalism. R.V.G. Clarke (editor), F.J. Gladstone, A. Sturman and Sheena Wilson (contributors). 1978. vi + 91pp. (0 11 340687 8).

48. Social inquiry reports: a survey. Jennifer Thorpe. 1979. vi + 55pp. (0 11 340688 6).

49. Crime in public view. P. Mayhew, R.V.G. Clarke, J.N. Burrows, J.M. Hough and S.W.C. Winchester. 1979. v + 36pp. (0 11 340689 4).

50. *Crime and the community. John Croft. 1979. v + 16pp. (0 11 340690 8).

51. Life-sentence prisoners. David Smith (editor), Christopher Brown, Joan Worth, Roger Sapsford and Charlotte Banks (contributors). 1979. iv + 51pp. (0 11 340691 6).

52. Hostels for offenders. Jane E. Andrews, with an appendix by Bill Sheppard. 1979. v + 30pp. (o 11 340692 4).

53. Previous convictions, sentence and reconviction: a statistical study of a sample of 5,000 offenders convicted in January 1971. G.J.O. Phillpotts and L.B. Lancucki, 1979. v + 55pp. (0 11 340693 2).

54. Sexual offences, consent and sentencing. Roy Walmsley and Karen White. 1979. vi + 77pp. (0 11 340694).

---

*Out of print.

55.   Crime prevention and the police. John Burrows, Paul Ekblom and Kevin Heal. 1979. v + 37pp. (0 11 340695 9).

56.   Sentencing practice in magistrates' courts. Roger Tarling, with the assistance of Mollie Weatheritt. 1979. vii + 54pp. (0 11 340696 7).

57.   Crime and comparative research. John Croft. 1979. iv + 16pp. (0 11 340697 5).

58.   Race, crime and arrests. Philip Stevens and Carole F. Willis. 1979. v + 69pp. (0 11 340698 3).

59.   Research and criminal policy. John Croft. 1980. iv + 14pp. (0 11 340699 1).

60.   Junior attendance centres. Anne B. Dunlop. 1980. v + 47pp. (0 11 340700 9).

61.   Police interrogation: an observational study in four police stations. Paul Softley, with the assistance of David Brown, Bob Forde, George Mair and David Moxon. 1980. vii + 67pp. (0 11 340701 7).

62.   Co-ordinating crime prevention efforts. F.J. Gladstone. 1980. v + 74pp. (0 11 340702 5).

63.   Crime prevention publicity: an assessment. D. Riley and P. Mayhew. 1980. v + 47pp. (0 11 340703 3).

64.   Taking offenders out of circulation. Stephen Brody and Roger Tarliong. 1980. v + 46pp. (0 11 340704 1).

65.   *Alcoholism and social policy: are we on the right lines? Mary Tuck. 1980. v + 30pp. (0 11 340705 X).

66.   Persistent petty offenders. Suzan Fairhead. 1981. vi + 78pp. (0 11 340706 8).

67.   Crime control and the police. Pauline Morris and Kevin Heal. 1981. v + 71pp. (0 11 340707 6).

68.   Ethnic minorities in Britain: a study of trends in their positions since 1961. Simon Field, George Mair, Tom Rees and Philip Stevens. 1981. v + 48pp. (0 11 340708 4).

69.   Managing criminological research. John Croft. 1981. iv + 17pp. (0 11 340709 2).

70.   Ethnic minorities, crime and policing: a survey of the experiences of West Indians and whites. Mary Tuck and Peter Southgate. 1981. iv + 54pp. (0 11 340765 3).

71.   Contested trials in magistrates' courts. Julie Vennard. 1982. v + 32pp. (0 11 340766 1).

72.   Public disorder: a review of research and a study in one inner city area. Simon Field and Peter Southgate. 1982. v + 77pp. (0 11 340767 X).

73.   Clearing up crime. John Burrows and Roger Tarling. 1982. vii + 31pp. (0 11 340768 8).

74.   Residential burglary: the limits of prevention. Stuart Winchester and Hilary Jackson. 1982. v + 47pp. (0 11 340769 6).

75.   Concerning crime. John Croft. 1982. iv + 16pp. (0 11 340770 X).

76.   The British Crime Survey: first report. Mike Hough and Pat Mayhew. 1983. v + 62pp. (0 11 340789 6).

77.   Contacts between police and public findings from the British Crime Survey. Peter Southgate and Paul Ekblom. 1984. v + 42pp. (0 11 340771 8).

78.   Fear of crime in England and Wales. Michael Maxfield. 1984. v + 51pp. (0 11 340772 6).

79.   Crime and police effectiveness. Ronald V. Clarke and Mike Hough. 1984. iv + 33pp. (0 11 340773 4).

80.` The attitudes of ethnic minorities. Simon Field. 1984. v + 50pp. (0 11 340774 2).

81.   Victims of crime: the dimensions of risk. Michael Gottfredson. 1984. V + 54pp. (0 11 340775 0).

82.   The tape-recording of police interviews with suspects. Carole Willis. 1984. v + 44pp. (0 11 340776 9).

ALSO

Designing out crime. R.V.G. Clarke and P. Mayhew (editors). 1980. vii + 186pp. (0 11 340732 7). (This book collects, with an introduction, studies that were originally published in HORS 34, 47, 49, 55, 62 and 63 and which are illustrative of the 'situational' approach to crime prevention).

The above HMSO publications can be purchased from Government Bookshops or through booksellers.

---

*Out of print.

The following Home Office research publications are availabale on request from the Home Office Research and Planning Unit, 50 Queen Anne's Gate, London, SW1H 9AT.

Research Unit Papers (RUP)

1. Uniformed police work and management technology. J.M. Hough. 1980

2. Supplementary information on sexual offences and sentencing. Roy Walmsley and Karen White. 1980.

3. Board of visitor adjudications. David Smith. Claire Austin and John Ditchfield. 1981.

4. Day centres and probations. Suzan Fairhead, with the assistance of J. Wilkinson-Grey. 1981.

Research and Planning Unit Papers (RPUP)

5. Ethnic minorities and complainst against the police. Philip Stevens and Carole Willis. 1982.

6. Crime and public housing. Mike Hough and Pat Mayhew (editors). 1982.

7. Abstracts of race relations research. George Mair and Philip Stevens (editors). 1982.

8. Police probationer training in race relations. Peter Southgate. 1982.

9. The police response to calls from the public. Paul Ekblom and Kevin Heal. 1982.

10. City centre crime: a situational approach to prevention. Malcolm Ramsay. 1982.

11. Burglary in schools: the prospects for prevention. Tim Hope. 1982.

12. Fire enforcement. Paul Softley and David Moxon. 1982.

13. Vietnamese refugees. Peter Jones. 1982.

14. Community resources for victims of crime. Karen Williams. 1983.

15. The use, effectiveness and impact of police stop and search powers. Carole Willis. 1983.

16. Acquittal rates. Sid Butler. 1983.

17. Criminal justice comparisons: the case of Scotland and England and Wales. Lorna J.F. Smith. 1983.

18. Time taken to deal with juveniles under criminal proceedings. Catherine Frankenburg and Roger Tarling. 1983.

19. Civilian review of complaints against the police: a survey of the United States literature. David C. Brown. 1983.

20. Police action on motoring offences. David Riley. 1983.

21. Diverting drunks from the criminal justice system. Sue Kingsley and George Mair. 1983.

22. The staff resource implications of an independent prosecution system. Peter R. Jones. 1983.

23. Reducing the prison population: an explantory study in Hampshire. David Smith, Bill Sheppard, George Mair and Karen Williams. 1984.

24. Criminal justice system model: magistrates' courts sub-model. Susan Rice. 1984.

25. Measures of police effectiveness and efficiency. Ian Sinclair and Clive Miller. 1984.

26. Punishment practice by prison Boards of Visitors. Susan Iles, Adrienne Connors, Chris May, Joy Mott. 1984.

27. Reparation, conciliations and mediation. Tony Marshall. 1984.

28. Magistrates' domestic courts: new perspectives. Tony Marshall (editor). 1984.

29. Racism awareness training for the police. Peter Southgate. 1984.

30. Community constables: a study of a policing initiative. David Brown and Susan Iles. 1985.

Research Bulletin

The Research Bulletin is published twice a year and consists mainly of short articles relating to projects which are part of the Home Office Research and Planning Unit's research programme.

Printed in the UK for HMSO, Dd.737574, C13, 2/85, 5673, 4675.